The 500cc World
Champions

Also by Michael Scott

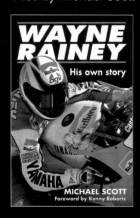

The 500cc World
Champions

THE STORY OF THE CLASS OF KINGS

Michael Scott *Foreword by Kenny Roberts*

First published in March 2002
Reprinted August 2002

A catalogue record for this book is
available from the British Library

ISBN 1 85960 845 0

Library of Congress catalog card no. 2001132576

Haynes North America Inc.,
861 Lawrence Drive, Newbury Park,
California 91320, USA.

Page-build by
G&M, Raunds, Wellingborough, Northamptonshire.

Published by Haynes Publishing, Sparkford,
Yeovil, Somerset BA22 7JJ, UK.

Tel: 01963 442030 Fax: 01963 440001
Int.tel: +44 1963 442030 Int.fax: +44 1963 440001
E-mail: sales@haynes-manuals.co.uk
Web site: www.haynes.co.uk

Printed and bound in Britain by
J.H. Haynes & Co. Ltd, Sparkford

Contents

Acknowledgements

Firstly, the author needs to thank the World Champions, who have not only achieved inspiring results, but have given him their time and their honesty over the years, and during preparation of this book. Many others have been helpful: especially Stuart and Chris Graham, sons of Les, also his close friend Alan Collinson, and former racers including Bill Lomas, Jim Redman, and Jack Findlay. Alan Robinson's contacts and detailed knowledge were invaluable; Iain Mackay has been a steadfast friend and source of first-hand anecdotes. Italian journalist Carlo Perelli and Gilera race-team boss Giampiero Sacchi also filled in many gaps; likewise many other friends and colleagues too numerous to mention.

This book would not have been possible without the help and co-operation of Dutch photographer Henk Keulemans, for whom nothing was too much trouble, and whose sense and knowledge of history are acute; likewise Swiss photographer Maurice Büla, who has photographed motorcycle racing since even before the championship was founded; and Nick Nicholls who also provided many early photographs. Thank you all.

Foreword

by three times World Champion Kenny Roberts Snr

Kenny Roberts became a campaigner against dangerous race-tracks. This is Imatra in 1979 – a particular target for criticism. (Henk Keulemans)

'**Ten cents and the World Championship** won't buy you a cup of coffee.' I said that back in the Eighties, to somebody who was trying to talk my history up, and not everybody understood. Some people thought I was knocking Grand Prix racing, and putting down the series.

Not so. I was just putting what I had done into some kind of proportion. It was the simple truth, and it's still the case. Winning the championship has nothing to do with financial gain, and everything to do with personal satisfaction. To me I could sum it all up in one corner: the left-hander before Stowe at Silverstone. For the first couple of laps, before the tyres went off, I could take it flat out. That feeling was everything about racing a 500.

The only person I wanted to please when I raced was myself. I started out – at 14 – to be the best. The only way you can say that you are the best is to be the World Champion. That's what allows you to say it.

To me, winning the actual championship was always anticlimactic. The next day I'd still be driving my motorhome back to the workshop in Amsterdam. The satisfaction comes from achieving what you've wanted to do.

I just wanted to be better than everybody else. That's why I sometimes rode machines that my competitors or even my crew chief Kel Carruthers said were uncompetitive. To win on those bikes was a personal test in pushing my skills to their very limits. Each time I accomplished this, my desire was fuelled to take those skills to

Two generations, three champions: Kenny Roberts Senior is joined on the Imola rostrum in 1983 by future 500 champion Kenny Junior. Freddie Spencer, on the right, has just won the title from Roberts. (Henk Keulemans)

another level, building even more confidence. My first World Championship was the end result. From that point on, exploring my abilities to extract the most from my equipment and myself became as rewarding as my subsequent titles.

There are a lot of riders with the ability to win races, who don't have the perseverance to deliver when conditions are not optimal. Winning the championship is a matter of having all the ingredients – you need the right factory support, the riding ability, the staying power ... and the want. That combination is what makes a great rider, and great riders don't come along that often.

I'm not sure how it felt to the other guys featured in this excellent book. I've met many of them, raced against some of them, and trained a few more. One of them is my own son – and I'm proud of how he endured the pressures of achieving his championship. Nobody who wins the 500 title does so without extremely hard work, mental toughness, and being a great rider.

The 500cc champions have one other thing in common. Without it, all you can say is that you used to race motorcycles. We can say we used to be World Champions, in the greatest racing class there was at that time.

Modesto, California
January 2002

Preface

The foundation of the World Championship in the post-war Europe of 1949 gave a new summit of achievement for motorcycle racers. The 500cc class was the highest peak. The first ever 500cc World Championship was won by an English bomber pilot on a thundering AJS. A new era of

motorcycle racing had begun. Fifty three years later that era was ended. New regulations consigned the half-litre heroes to history. And a line of twenty-two 500cc champions – including the greatest names in racing – was completed in 2001 by a cheeky young Italian riding a brutally shrieking high-tech two-stroke Honda.

These champions are the cream of the cream. Even here, there is an elite. Winning once is a considerable achievement. Then there are those – not satisfied with the first ascent – who won the title again and again. And who didn't give up, in many cases, until they were physically ruined.

By 2001, the GP series had grown from six to 16 races, and spanned the globe. Sixteen punishing occasions when a would-be champion must plunder his resources to put himself somehow above the best riders on the best motorcycles in the world. The physical and mental dedication required is draining – 500cc riders tend to age rapidly. The depth of commitment needed to contest the title year after year is of another order entirely.

It is fascinating to speculate at what point talent and determination become obsession, and at what point obsession becomes madness. For dedication at this level – to the exclusion of almost everything else – is sufficiently far from normal behaviour to be categorised as crazy, if not necessarily insane. This is true of any sport. The danger endemic to motorcycle racing adds another level. To these Olympians, the price of failure can go far beyond mere public humiliation.

Madness it must be. But to those who practise 500 GP racing, and to

In his third title year, Eddie Lawson pushes Yamaha team-mate Didier de Radigues back to their pit by scooter power. (Henk Keulemans)

Spain's only 500 champion Alex Criville learned from Mick Doohan, and it paid off when his team-mate retired hurt. (Henk Keulemans)

those who follow the sport, this is a fine and a particularly courageous kind of madness, combining the fluid grace and freedom of motorcycling with levels of power and performance so brutish that it takes a near superman just to hang on. In this world, the champions stand head and shoulders above the merely excellent.

This book marks the passing of the classic 500 class by celebrating the riders who have led the way. The engine size defined the motorcycles, but was the men who made the championship.

Vaulting technical progress has advanced the 500cc racing motorcycle of 2001 far beyond those now clumsy-looking paragons of 1949. The changes – almost four times the horsepower, plus slick tyres – make it impossible to compare the required riding techniques. It is futile to try to rate the skills of the first champion Les Graham against those of Valentino Rossi in 2001.

The spirit of victory is probably little different, however. Just, perhaps, more intense. For the first 25 of the 500cc years, riders competed not only in other GP classes, but also in a number of international races. For the final 15 years of the class, with just one exception, 500cc Grand Prix racers have concentrated on one class, and (but for rare excursions beyond) on GPs alone.

The exception was American Freddie Spencer who, in 1985, claimed both the 250 and 500cc titles. He accomplished this in the second year of my attendance at every GP. His brief and brilliant GP career coincided with the start of my own as a World Championship-dedicated journalist.

In my first full season I'd got to know Freddie, as well as that year's winner Eddie Lawson. My previous work in motorcycle journalism had already brought me into regular professional contact and on first-name terms with earlier stars: Barry Sheene, Kenny Roberts, Phil Read and Mike

What *is the* Championship?

There were never any mysteries about how to operate a championship – scores are awarded for race positions, then at the end of each season the rider with the most points wins. Variations introduced from the start of the 500 series, however, meant that this wasn't necessarily the case – the first title went to British rider Les Graham, even though he had scored only 31 points in total compared with Gilera rival Nello Pagani's 40. The apparent anomaly is the result of a secondary system, whereby points were counted from only three of the six races that season. With only the best results taken into account,

Graham had 30 points to Pagani's 29.

This system of counting only the best scores protected otherwise good riders who might miss a win or two because of mechanical failure or injury. It also meant that a rider might tie up the title by winning all the opening rounds, and then stay home for the rest of the year.

It remained in place from 1949 until 1976, when it was finally dropped, so that all the races counted. In 1991, the system was reintroduced for just one year, allowing riders to drop one result from the 15 races. It made no difference to the final outcome, and was dropped again.

A much earlier casualty was the extra point for fastest lap of the race, a bonus that was on offer only for the first season.

Early on, points were much harder to come by, however. In 1949, only the top five finishers got points, increased to the top six from 1950 until 1968, when points were paid through to 10th place. From 1988 until the present day, the top 15 finishers earn points, again with a one-year aberration when, in 1992, the number was cut to ten. From 1993, the current points system (25-20-16-13-11-10-9-8-7-6-5-4-3-2-1) was adopted.

Hailwood. As a youth I'd met Gary Hocking. Now at the circuits I started to spend time with Yamaha team manager Giacomo Agostini. Then I met John Surtees, and a while later worked with Geoff Duke.

At the races, Marco Lucchinelli was still active – and Franco Uncini is still working in GP racing (as safety officer) today. New candidates were constantly joining the orbit: combative Wayne Gardner, friendly Wayne Rainey, ebullient Kevin Schwantz, at-first diffident Mick Doohan. Alex Criville was rising through the 125 ranks; Kenny Roberts Junior and then Valentino Rossi were on the way.

As the class drew to its close, it became obvious that it was the right time for this book. Scanning the list of winners, I realised that – with the exception of Umberto Masetti – I had already met all of the surviving World Champions. This rare privilege made it as much a duty as a pleasure to chronicle, and bring up to date, the individual stories of the men who made the championship mean so much.

Time spent with champions also gave me a detached observer's insight into the very disparate characters of these men, all vastly different from one another, but with a single common thread – that obsessive,

The icons have it. Duke with Agostini at the 1991 TT. (Phil Masters)

When Valentino Rossi moved to Honda in 2000 he took over Doohan's team, his bike, and his mantle – and added a whole new sense of fun. (Henk Keulemans)

The series had come a long way since that first championship won by Les Graham. (Graham Family Archive)

incomprehensible determination. That fine madness. A madness that they do not acknowledge while in its grip, but from which they tend to feel released, eventually, when it is all over.

There is something else upon which they tend to agree: that the championship in itself did not have a great deal of meaning. Especially to the riders of the modern era – who were less sporting, perhaps, and more ruthlessly professional, than their predecessors. The title was not central to their obsession, but a more or less useful adjunct, if only as a yardstick for outsiders to know their ability. Their own satisfaction was in achieving personal best, usually (though not always) marked by winning individual races. It may be akin to a rich man scorning the value of money, but many of the serial champions talk of a sense of anti-climax on actually winning the crown. This was a feeling so puzzling to triple-champion Wayne Rainey that it drove him to strive still harder to achieve the ultimate again, in order to try to understand more about that strange, unexpected feeling of letdown.

To five-times champion Mick Doohan, famously matter of fact about these things, winning meant that 'you get to stick the Number 1 on the front of your bike the next year where you can't even see it – but it makes you a target for everyone else'. More important to him was 'the instant gratification of winning a race'.

To Giacomo Agostini, the man who won more 500-class championships than anybody, victory was for many years a duty – a necessary fulfilment of his talent which had already put him on an infinitely superior machine. Then, when things went wrong at MV Agusta, winning became a personal statement again. To Surtees, it was all a bit too easy – and something that stood in the way of the stronger desire to win race after race, since his MV Agusta contract prevented him from racing as often as he wanted in non-championship events.

The making of a champion requires certain ingredients: the right team, the right motorcycle, the right sponsor. It is often a mark of a rider's determination as well as talent that these three come together at the right time. Just part of getting to the top.

Self-belief goes without saying. In this sort of company, nobody succeeds unless they are totally sure of their ability to do so. Suzuki team manager Garry Taylor explains that commitment and consistency were two of the main characteristics he looked for in hiring new riders – champions Kevin Schwantz and Kenny Roberts Junior are two of Taylor's recruits. 'Everyone arrives in the 500 class wanting to be World Champion,' he said. 'If after two years they still believe they can do it, and if that is a realistic belief, then they are halfway there.'

The most crucial element a rider must supply is what several have called 'The Want'. It is a matter of total focus and complete dedication. Kenny Roberts Senior recalls how he realised these commodities were in limited supply, even before his personal store ran out. 'If you have the slightest element of doubt, then you cannot make the commitment you need. I had always said that when I went to bed or woke up and I wasn't thinking about how to improve my lap time, then I'm out of here. When you no longer sleep, breath and eat racing – you have to quit.'

This book then is about 22 men who slept, breathed and ate motorcycle racing – to better effect than any of their rivals.

Introduction

Why 500cc? Why not 600? 1,000? Or even 50 good old American cubic inches? The choice was refreshingly whimsical, at a time when the whole internal combustion idea was still somewhat new-fangled, and engines were more usually defined by their number of cylinders, or arbitrary horsepower ratings based on the cylinder bore rather than by swept volume. The 500 class came into being largely because it was a nice round number. By the time the World Championship series began in 1949, 500s had been at the apex of racing for more than 30 years.

When the class was born, as now, 500cc was not an optimal capacity, or the peak of the two-wheel experience. Road-going sports motorcycles regularly ran (and run) to more than double that size. By 1949, 500cc was a

AJS won the first 500cc championship in 1949, but struggled to keep their twin-cylinder 500 competitive. This 1954 version had slanted cylinders and conventional cooling fins – but the Porcupine nickname stuck.
(Nick Nicholls)

popular capacity for a serious sporting road bike, more a result of the well-established 500 class than the other way around.

The first 500s raced at the Isle of Man Tourist Trophy. It was in 1909, the third running of the TT, that a 500cc limit was pioneered, as a way of giving parity to the two classes already existing, for twin- and single-cylinder motorcycles. At the time, the singles were rather better at what was already turning from reliability trial to road race. Twins were favoured with an upper limit of 750cc. The singles were pegged at 500cc. A breed was born. Year by year, the size of the twins was cut back until by 1912, the second year when two races were run under the Senior and Junior titles, the Seniors were 500cc and the Juniors 350cc, no matter how many cylinders were employed. The true 500 class had arrived.

It was more than 60 years before the TT was dethroned as a centrepiece of the World Championships. By 1977 the road course was considered too dangerous. The new British GP ran on the mainland, at Silverstone. The 500cc legacy lasted rather longer – just ten years short of a full century – the premier racing class from 1912 to 2001.

The reign of the 500s was ended by decree, at the behest of the major factories who were concerned at the growing distance between their large-capacity four-stroke sports motorcycles and the specialist two-stroke GP 500s. GP racing, while as fascinating and as expensive as ever, was out on a limb.

The rescue plan was radical. From 2002, new rules would open the class to four-stroke prototypes of up to 990cc. The old 500s would be eligible too, but the 500 class as such was consigned to history. This book celebrates that history.

Always fast, 500 racing was not always glamorous. Triple champion Kenny Roberts leads the tyre-trolley and rival Boet van Dulmen through Finland's primitive paddock in 1979.
(Henk Keulemans)

The mid-Seventies saw huge crowds as the two-stroke era began. Here, the MV Agustas of Phil Read and Franco Bonera lead Barry Sheene's two-stroke Suzuki at Eau Rouge at Spa in Belgium in 1975.
(Henk Keulemans)

The 500cc limit had seen many variations, ranging from Norton's definitive bevel-drive overhead camshaft single-cylinder Manx to the vaulting ambition of Moto Guzzi designer Giulio Carcano's V8. That particular flight of fancy died when the Italian factories (except for MV Agusta) withdrew en masse at the end of 1957, citing rising costs and falling sales. Any would-be successors were effectively buried in 1968 when a regulation change, intended to cut soaraway costs, limited the maximum number of cylinders to four.

This left the four-strokes hamstrung as the new breed of high-performance two-strokes, already dominant in the smaller classes, mounted a serious invasion. By the mid-Seventies, the battle had been won. Howling and warbling, the MVs had provided glamorous aural counterpoint to the die-hard singles. As the bell-bottom Sixties merged into the platform-flared Seventies, the buzz-saw screech of the two-strokes took over the score for the final movement of the 500-class opera.

Four-strokes were never banned from the class – they just ran out of power, a situation only emphasised when Honda made a technically adventurous but ultimately embarrassing attack at the end of the Seventies. Their ambitious 32-valve NSR V4 had unique oval-pistons, making it a quasi V8. The bike had trouble even qualifying. Two-strokes have powered every 500-class World Champion since 1975.

Some die-hard fans believed that the 500s of the turn of the new millennium were the ultimate racing motorcycle, and that the new big-bore four-strokes – heavier and more powerful – would simply shred their tyres trying to keep up with these paragons. (Some thought the same of the MV Agusta, when the two-strokes came.) Others are more confident that the

Tension released with plastic cups and horseplay: new 1982 champion Franco Uncini (centre) plays hostage to team-mate Loris Reggiani's unconvincing attack on hapless Suzuki engineer Mitsu Okamoto. (Henk Keulemans)

Clash of the giants, 1983 San Marino GP – Roberts (4), Spencer (3), Lucchinelli (5), Mamola (6), Lawson (27). (Henk Keulemans)

numbers will rule – the greater potential power of the bigger engines will win in the end.

All that remained to be seen. What was certain, at the end of the 2001 season, was that the true 500 championship was over. This was the end of an era that had begun soon after the dawn of bike racing.

The idea of combining points gained in the classic Grand Prix races of the so-called Continental Circus (including the TT, the German GP at the Nürburgring, Monza in Italy and Assen in Holland) actually began in 1939, just before the start of the Second World War. It was called the European, rather than the World, Championship (a notion American maverick Kenny Roberts would later agree with), but the first year of the new title was cut short by the start of hostilities, with Georg Meier's BMW heading the table at the time. The young men in leathers returned home to start fighting one another in earnest – at least one of them, popular English rider Les Graham, served heroically, and won the DFC as a bomber pilot.

Four years after peace returned to a ravaged Europe, in 1949, the series began properly. The first winner was that same Les Graham, on the AJS. And this time, the title was World Champion.

Graham was the first of twenty-two 500-class champions – men from six different nations, and with widely different temperaments and characters. All they had in common was a will to win so passionate and so constant that it could carry them through a full season of superiority over a group of individuals who each had the same burning desire.

The cast that assembled for the start of the series was a mix of old (pre-war) and new riders, and of old and new bikes. Graham's closest rival for

Spencer was the youngest ever champion at 21. He looks his age, on the rostrum with defeated 1983 rivals Marco Lucchinelli (left) and Ron Haslam. (Henk Keulemans)

Push-start racing lasted until the mid-Eighties – here Randy Mamola (3), Eddie Lawson (4), Raymond Roche (11) and Ron Haslam (9) flex their muscles for the off in Sweden in 1984. (Henk Keulemans)

the first title was Nello Pagani on the Gilera, and new Gilera team rider Umberto Masetti won in 1950 and 1952, with Geoff Duke in between with the one and only Norton crown, before he too switched to Gilera and a hat-trick of wins.

It was another great Englishman who brought in the next dominant marque – MV Agusta. Future F1 car champion John Surtees won his first 500 crown in 1956, conceded to Libero Liberati's Gilera in 1957, then swept – invincible – to three titles in a row. This was the start of 17 years of complete domination by the MVs: after Surtees came Gary Hocking, for just one year, followed by Mike Hailwood for the next four. Then the most decorated rider in the 500-class, Giacomo Agostini, swept to seven of his eight 500 titles in a blur of red and a howl of sweet exhaust music. Honda and Hailwood challenged hard, but by the end the opposition comprised mainly distant privateers on grumblingly outpaced single-cylinder machines.

Ago was ousted by Phil Read, who won twice on the MV in 1973 and 1974. And that was the end of the famous fire engine.

The honour of riding Yamaha's first winning two-stroke went to none other than Agostini. This was some kind of a change for the all-Italian hero, but his relations with MV had soured after the arrival of Read, and this narrow victory over his great rival represented a revenge that was both sweet and historic.

Barry Sheene came next – a natural star whose personality widened the appeal of bike racing in Britain as he became a household name. His Suzuki won twice, before quick-draw US champion Kenny Roberts swaggered into town. The first American to become 500cc World Champion mounted a formidable assault to win three times in a row for

A golden age of 500cc racing. The field at the 1990 US GP may have been small, but look at the quality. Schwantz (34), Doohan (9), Gardner (10) and Rainey (2) lead the field from the Laguna Seca start line. (Henk Keulemans)

Yamaha, faltering thereafter to give two more Suzuki titles to Italians Marco Lucchinelli and Franco Uncini.

Then came another crucial moment as yet another American came to continue the takeover. This time it was Freddie Spencer, and 1983 was an epic year as Fast Freddie narrowly defeated King Kenny for Honda's long-awaited first-ever title in the class of kings. At 21, Spencer beat Hailwood by one year to become the youngest ever 500 champion.

Kenny's Yamaha replacement Eddie Lawson doggedly defeated Spencer in 1984 as Honda had a bad bike year with their new V4. In 1985 it was the other way round – and Spencer won the 250 crown as well. Then Lawson again, followed by the bullish Australian Wayne Gardner (Honda) before Lawson once again took his Yamaha turn. Then Steady Eddie jumped ship, moving unexpectedly to Honda to take a second title in succession in 1989. Only Duke and Agostini had won on different makes before, and neither of them back-to-back.

The American domination was challenged by a handful of bright Australians. From 1978 to 1989 Americans won nine times, Italians twice, and an Australian once. It wasn't over yet. The run of US riders was to continue for the next four years straight, as Wayne Rainey and Kevin Schwantz brought their bitter US Championship double-act to the world stage.

Rainey won three times and was leading year four when he was crippled by a late-season crash in Italy. That crown went to Schwantz, who memorably said: 'I'd rather not be champion than for Wayne to be in a

Racing's down side. Obsession with winning drove Wayne Rainey to disaster. Shocked mechanics wheel the bike away after his crippling crash at Misano in 1993.
(Henk Keulemans)

Mick Doohan fought back from injury and dominated for five straight years. (Henk Keulemans)

wheelchair.' It brought to an end a golden age, with Gardner and Lawson always in the frame, and the incoming Mick Doohan rapidly gaining strength.

Doohan might have been champion before 1994 but for serious leg injuries in 1992. Certainly nobody else could be champion once he had taken over. Mick held off all comers for the next five years in a magisterial display of control – over his NSR Honda and over his cowed rivals. It was ended only by a crash in the third round of the 1999 season. At that point he was trailing on points to upstart Kenny Roberts Junior on the Suzuki, but it was Mick's team-mate Alex Criville who came through to win the title, the first Spaniard to do so. The next year Roberts would not be denied, claiming the first father-and-son title in this or any other class for his now dynastic family.

The last year of the 500 class – the last 16 of 580 GPs – was, fittingly, an epic. Among the records broken was that for the closest-ever finish in the class: the first nine riders within 2.8 seconds at the Australian GP. The winner of this breathtaking celebration of 500cc GP racing, tooth and nail, on the limit, was Valentino Rossi. It was the ninth of 11 wins for him that year. And it was enough, by inches, to give the Honda rider the title, from defeated rival Max Biaggi's Yamaha.

Rossi was already 125 and 250 champion, and a hero beyond the shores of his native Italy, and outside the narrow confines of the world of motorcycle racing. He won the title magnificently, fighting all the way for the right to be the last 500cc World Champion.

Kenny Roberts Jnr put the family name on the 500 roll of honour for a fourth time – the only father-son combination in GP racing. (Henk Keulemans)

Valentino Rossi, favourite of the gods, who won the last-ever championship bearing the magic number 500. (Henk Keulemans)

Les **Graham**

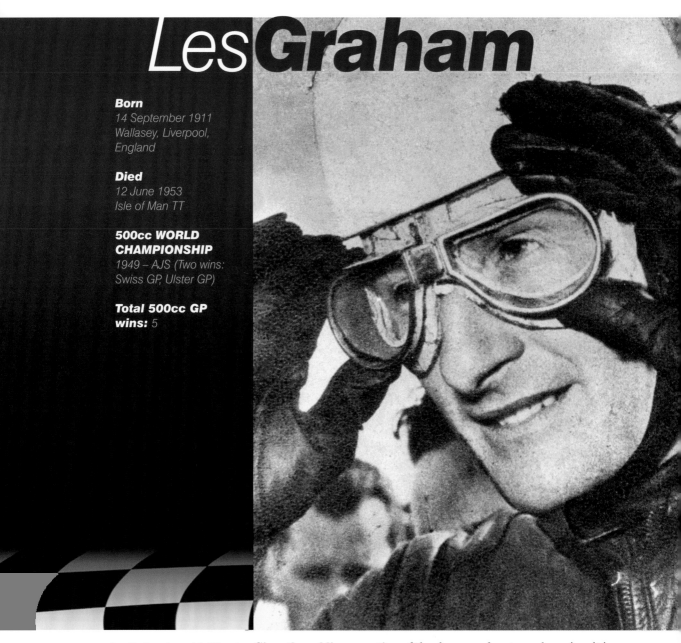

Born
14 September 1911
Wallasey, Liverpool,
England

Died
12 June 1953
Isle of Man TT

**500cc WORLD
CHAMPIONSHIP**
1949 – AJS (Two wins:
Swiss GP, Ulster GP)

**Total 500cc GP
wins:** 5

*Les Graham brought skill and
experience to the first 500 title, which
he won at the age of 38.* (Maurice Büla)

Given the public perception of the dangers of motorcycle racing, it is a
remarkable fact that of the 22 winners in the 500 class, only one lost his life
in a motorcycle racing accident. Les Graham is that man – the first World
Champion, the first of a string of British champions, a graduate from the
old school of racers, and one of nature's gentlemen.

Graham was obviously a remarkable person. Every photograph shows
him smiling, every personal recollection brings forth the same comment:
'Oh, he was a lovely man.' This I have heard from friends, rivals, sponsors
… everyone who knew him, it seems. According to a close friend Alan
Collinson, competitions manager for Ferodo Brake Linings at the time,
'everybody worshipped him.'

The standard bearer of the new school, Geoff Duke, commented in his

First champion and a first-class gentleman

autobiography that Graham was not just a target for new riders in the championship that had grown out of the Continental Circus, but also a kindly mentor, and 'a thorough sportsman', who heartily congratulated Duke when the rising new boy beat him for the first time at one of the post-war international meetings.

Graham had a long racing career that began before the war when, as a Dot rider, he was described as an 'also-ran'. He'd been a member of the Continental Circus, working for OK Supreme as a development rider and racer.

Then came the war – and the perfect role for a gallant and daring motorcycle racer was as a pilot in the RAF. Not in a fighter, however. Acting Flight Lieutenant Robert Leslie Graham instead flew heavyweight Lancaster bombers, with four big V12 Merlin engines and a crew of seven. And with distinction. He was decorated on 8 December 1944 with the Distinguished Flying Cross, for general valour. 'He never spoke about it – he'd just say they had a few left over, or they'd posted it to him by mistake,' said his son Stuart Graham, himself a successful motorcycle and car racer; but Stuart did hear his late mother Edna tell of one incident when, after a high-risk bombing raid on U-boat pens in France, his father had stayed on behind to photograph the damage, a sitting-duck single target.

Stuart, the elder of two brothers, was 11 years old when his father was

Graham's long racing career began before the Second World War, and resumed with AJS. This is his title-winning 'Porcupine' of 1949. (Maurice Büla)

Graham is remembered as a kind mentor and a thorough sportsman. (Maurice Büla)

killed at the Isle of Man at the start of his third season with MV Agusta. The family had moved to Italy the previous winter, and until that point Stuart remembers the fun and glamour of the motorcycle racing life, but not much detail. When they lived in Kent, near AJS, young Stuart would wait by the gate for a lift up the driveway on the front mudguard. Later, he would ride round the paddock on the tank of the MV 500. There was the villa in Italy, dinners with Count Agusta, and races all over Europe. Then, suddenly, Les was gone. The older Stuart gets the more he regrets that he only ever had the chance to know his father as a child.

At the birth of the 500cc championships, Graham was aged 38. However he had a major advantage over the new generation of racing rivals – experience, of riding, race-craft, and machine development. A smooth, stylish and forceful rider, he'd signed up with AJS directly after the war to race their new twin-cylinder Porcupine 500. The combination stormed to victory against the strong challenge of the faster but relatively heavy multi-cylinder Gileras, and the lithe but slower single-cylinder Nortons. Graham won two races that season, narrowly outpointing Nello Pagani on the Gilera. There were only six rounds, but these were long, hard races. The Isle of Man TT lasted two hours and 50 minutes, covering almost 265 miles (Les's AJS broke down on the last lap, when he had a lead of 90 seconds); the Dutch TT was a two-hour 185-mile marathon. Today's GPs seldom last much longer than 40 minutes.

The famous Graham Grin was broad after his inaugural victory, and smiled out from Craven A cigarette advertisements. The smile grew strained over the following year, with frustration at the lack of development and poor reliability of the AJS. His frustration was relieved by Count Agusta who invited the British veteran to join his still formative racing team, and to help develop their powerful but clumsy four-cylinder 500 – an awkwardly innovative machine with odd parallelogram rear suspension and girder forks, both with torsion-bar springs. Although success was elusive in 1951, the British bomber pilot played a key role in the early evolution of the MV into the most successful four-stroke in 500 class history.

Graham won MV's first 500 race in Switzerland in 1952, finishing a close second overall once again to Masetti on the Gilera. He returned on the now considerably refined and much more conventional machine in 1953 but, in the first round of the new season, one day after winning his first ever TT on the 125 MV, he crashed fatally on the second lap of the Senior race. The loss of this revered rider was a sad blow to fans and to the sport.

How did it happen? There were some suggestions of steering failure … a broken bolt. Others tell of how he had just received a pit signal that Duke

Graham on the MV, airborne at the Ulster GP in 1952. The Earles front fork he favoured was an elegant but heavy design.
(Graham Family Archive)

One last race start – Graham pushes the MV away for the 1953 Senior TT. He crashed fatally on the second lap. (Maurice Büla)

was ahead of him by (at the end of that lap) almost 40 seconds. Dismayed, Graham howled off down Bray Hill at unprecedented speed. At the bottom, he crashed.

Friend, rival and junior MV team-mate Bill Lomas blames Graham's own unconventional choice of an Earles front fork. Made in Britain, these forks offered some advantages in steering and braking in exchange for a much heavier steered weight. They worked superbly at the smooth Monza circuit, and Graham was convinced of their superiority, says Lomas.

'I tried a bike with them fitted at the Ulster GP. On the seven-mile-long Clady straight, where you were jumping three feet off the ground at 150mph, it would get into such a tank-slapper – a pendulum effect. I told them to take them off, and fit telescopic forks, and it handled perfectly. But Les liked them.'

Graham's accident was probably triggered by a tank-slapper that started on landing from the hump later dubbed Ago's Leap. The big four swerved at high speed over the kerb and into the wall on the left-hand side and ricocheted across the road. Graham was killed instantly.

Stuart Graham grew up to race motorcycles himself, earning a place in the Suzuki factory team, and repeating his father's feat of winning an Isle of Man TT. He moved into car racing, winning the British Saloon Car title twice in the mid-Seventies in a Chevrolet Camaro, and driving for Ford as well. He also won the four-wheel version of the Isle of Man TT – the only man to win there on two and four wheels. His father had been destined to drive for the Jaguar sports car team the year he died.

The Isle of Man has an official Les Graham memorial, a famous landmark on a fast stretch up the mountain. He will be remembered always as the first World Champion. And also, by those lucky enough to know him, as the racer who everybody loved.

He won MV Agusta's first GP after joining the new Italian contenders to help develop their four-cylinder racer. Here he exercises the machine at a pre-season street race at Ferrarra in 1953.
(Graham Family Archive)

Les Graham, with his wife Edna.
(Graham Family Archive)

Umberto Masetti

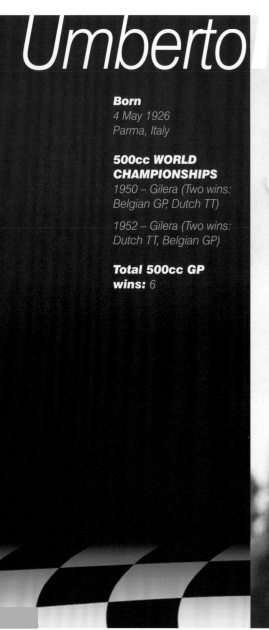

Born
4 May 1926
Parma, Italy

500cc WORLD CHAMPIONSHIPS
1950 – Gilera (Two wins: Belgian GP, Dutch TT)

1952 – Gilera (Two wins: Dutch TT, Belgian GP)

Total 500cc GP wins: 6

A man with dashing good looks and a passionate Italian nature, Umberto Masetti was a surprise to himself and others. (Maurice Büla)

A contemporary book quotes an unexpected remark from the new World Champion Umberto Masetti at the end of the 1950 season in which his four-cylinder Gilera easily outperformed but only narrowly outpointed Duke's single-cylinder Norton to win the second ever 500 title. He said that racing motorcycles scared him, and he would prefer to race cars. He did later get a test for Ferrari but it came to nothing because he was just too busy racing bikes.

Reluctantly or not, Masetti went on to have a career as a professional World Championship motorcycle racer that would span another eight years in the GPs, and include another 500cc title two years later, as well as serial success in national Italian racing.

Then again, it's just the sort of surprising thing Masetti might have said

Erratic genius who was scared of bikes

without particularly meaning it. He was a man full of surprises, even to himself. To film-star good looks and a passionate Italian nature he added a wayward streak that was a key feature of a very erratic career, and a home life rather the same.

At the end of his tenure as a works rider, in a classic riches-to-rags fable, Masetti's fortunes continued to decline. The former factory star from Gilera and MV Agusta took a self-imposed exile to South America, leaving behind a complex tangle of personal relationships and ex-wives. The double World Champion continued to race in South America, during a dark period in what had once seemed a charmed life. He returned to Italy only in 1972, at the expense of the organisers of one of the first-ever parades of classic bikes and riders, at the Imola 200 race. Subsequently, he could be found filling petrol tanks at a motorway service station outside Modena.

Masetti, now fully retired, is seen from time to time as an honoured guest at various classic racing functions. It is right that he should be honoured – any man who beat Geoff Duke should be able to count on that, no matter what the circumstances.

On the Gilera, again unfaired, in Italy, 1952. (Maurice Büla)

In action on the Gilera in 1950 – Masetti made the most of the strengths of his four-cylinder racer. (Maurice Büla)

Umberto first raced in 1946, at the age of 20. As the son of the Parma agent for Gilera, he was well placed to come to the attention of the top factory's race-department luminary, ex rider and car racing star Piero Taruffi. He was taken into the factory team as a 24-year-old, graduating the next year from the single-cylinder Saturno to the four-cylinder factory racer, as team-mate to 1949 runner-up Nello Pagani and the glamorous and daring Carlo Bandirola.

The Gilera firm traditionally eschewed the opening round at the Isle of Man TT, but Masetti achieved two crucial victories at the next two rounds in Belgium and Holland, where the challenging first-race winner Duke retired on both occasions with tyre problems. In Switzerland he was second to Graham's AJS with Duke fourth; the English rider's Norton won the next race at the notoriously bumpy Clady circuit outside Belfast – the Ulster TT. Duke won again at Monza, but Masetti's second place, less than ten seconds adrift in spite of being near collapse with influenza, was enough to give him the title by just one point. Some called him a lucky champion, gifted the title by Duke's tyre failures. Others just called him champion.

Duke made no mistake the next year, with Masetti claiming just one more win in the opening round in Spain, making the rostrum again in Ulster and at Monza, but with three no-scores: in Belgium, Assen (where he retired) and Switzerland, after a practice injury, he was third overall, behind Duke and new Gilera team-mate Alfredo Milani.

History had more in store for Masetti, for in 1952 he would become the first ever double champion. The opposition was slightly changed. Duke was still on the Norton, but now fighting a rearguard action on an outclassed machine, but the Gilera copies from Gallarate, the MV Agustas, had now reached a state of some maturity and posed a real threat in the hands of the crash-prone Bandirola and first champion Les Graham.

Masetti retired from the Swiss round and missed the TT. But then came a famous victory, against Duke at Assen: a track where the good handling of the Norton compensated somewhat for the lack of power – but not enough to prevent Masetti waving confidently to his pit on the last lap after a race-long duel, and finally opening the throttle all the way to cross the line just over one second ahead of his thwarted British rival.

Masetti exploited his extra power for a very similar result at Spa one week later. Two weeks after that, Duke was injured at Solitude in Germany, and while Masetti was also hurt in a crash at the same track, he was able to continue racing, finishing second at Monza – a full minute behind Les Graham, taking the first MV Agusta victory. They repeated this result at the final in Spain, and Masetti claimed a second championship from Graham by three points.

Masetti, riding high, was due for a fall. It came in the form of his new team-mate for 1953: unexpectedly, Gilera hired Geoff Duke. Masetti was severely upset at being partnered with such talent, and showed the world at the Dutch TT when, in practice, he was handsomely outpaced by the Englishman. The defending champion packed his bags and left before the race. He did much the same at Monza, and though he did win the Italian 500 title, he also earned the nickname 'The Invisible Masetti'.

He won his national title again in 1954, but was still smarting at his reduced status in the Gilera team. So the next year he switched camps, moving to MV to finish third overall in the world, winning an epic victory at home at Monza, the last GP of 1955, where he defeated the Gileras of Reg Armstrong and Duke by half-a-second and 1.6-seconds respectively.

Masetti stayed with MV until the end of 1958, when he retired from GP racing and subsequently left Italy, returning only in 1972, on an expenses-paid trip for a classic demonstration at the Imola 200-mile event.

'My biggest mistake,' he later told friends, 'was ever to leave Gilera.' But whether staying on would have made much difference to an erratic life of highs and lows, driven by talent and temperament in equal measure, is open to question.

Geoff Duke

Born
*29 March 1923
St Helens, Lancashire,
England*

**500cc WORLD
CHAMPIONSHIPS**
*1951 – Norton (Four wins:
Isle of Man TT, Belgian
GP, Dutch TT, Ulster GP)*

*1953 – Gilera (Four wins:
Dutch TT, French GP,
Swiss GP, Italian GP)*

*1954 – Gilera (Five wins:
Belgian GP, Dutch TT,
German GP, Swiss GP,
Italian GP)*

*1955 – Gilera (Four wins:
French GP, Isle of Man TT,
German GP, Dutch TT)*

**Total 500cc GP
wins:** *22*

Other titles
*1951 – 350cc World
Champion (Norton)*

*1952 – 350cc World
Champion (Norton)*

*The outwardly modest Lancastrian who
won his maiden 500 title on a Norton,
then switched to Gilera to become the
first serial World Champion.
(Nick Nicholls)*

This book is full of stories about children born into motorcycling families,
and what happened to them when they were steered into racing by
enthusiastic fathers and supportive mothers. Geoff Duke's story is
different. His love of motorcycling was entirely self-generated, his drive in
search of perfect performance entirely self-motivated.

This clean-cut and outwardly modest racer with a gentlemanly air, in a
post-war Britain where spectators at race-tracks still wore collar and tie,
became the first ever serial 500cc champion, the first ever double 350/500
champion and a TT master. His name was a byword for smooth, stylish
riding. He had no push from behind other than a passion triggered at the
age of 10 (he later wrote) by the bewitching smell of Castrol R racing oil,
followed by pillion rides on his older brother's machine to watch local

Icon who set the standard and upped the pace

sand-track racing on the broad beaches in the north west of England.

Self-taught? Or just a natural? Certainly Duke had a gift for making it all look easy, so elegant were his corner lines and so accurate his riding. Whether he was extracting the last tenth from the slower but better-handling Nortons, measuring out the power on the faster but clumsier Gileras with their big full streamlining, threading smoothly between the walls and hedges on the Isle of Man, or sweeping at speed through the trees at Spa or Monza, Duke was the rider who for more than five years set the standard and upped the pace.

This future icon of bike racing was born and raised in St Helens, outside Liverpool, where his father had a baking and confectionery business. Geoff was a pre-teen when his brother suffered serious injuries in a road crash, and the family feeling turned very much against motorcycling. Destiny will not be denied, however, and Duke's riding career began soon afterwards with a subterfuge. He and two friends pooled their saved pocket money and bought an aged belt-driven Raleigh motorcycle for ten shillings (which was scrap money even then, but literally translates as 50p), then came a 500cc Triumph for 15 shillings. They secretly rebuilt these and would ride them every weekend on a local farm, using an alarm clock as a stop-watch on their impromptu track. Geoff held the lap record. When his parents learned the truth they reluctantly accepted the situation. 'They were not happy … but presumably because I had not been hurt … did no more than plead with me to be very careful,' he wrote in his autobiography *In Pursuit of Perfection* (Osprey).

Duke bought his first road bike in 1940, a transport hack. More

Duke was soon a household name. When news broke that he was leaving Norton to ride for Gilera he'd had some explaining to do.
(Maurice Büla)

sporting riding followed a couple of years later, courtesy of the taxpayer. At this time, young men were required to do national service, and although his first application to be a dispatch rider with the Royal Corps of Signals was rejected, he found another way of performing his duty while at the same time enjoying motorcycling.

Determined to succeed, Duke joined the Corps as an instrument mechanic, then talked his way into a transfer to the motorcycling section, where he excelled. His gift saw him retained as an instructor, followed by a valuable time of mixed motorcycling ranging from army trials to stunt riding with the famous motorcycling display team. He left in 1947, immediately bought a mud-plugging trials bike, and started winning right away. It was in trials, he would later say, that he learned the precise throttle control that is the cornerstone of fast 500 riding. Trials were to riders of Duke's generation what oval dirt-tracks would later be to the American champions 20 years down the road.

Duke soon found himself employed by BSA as a trials rider, but he was keen to move into road racing, as well as to find a full-time job in a British motorcycle industry that was still thriving and had plenty of space for this personable young Lancastrian.

Duke was on the brink of joining AMC (Matchless, AJS *et al*) when an even better chance came up, in view of his road-racing ambitions … an invitation to join Norton. It was again as a trials rider, but the great racing factory viewed his tarmac ambitions with enthusiasm. It seems – certainly in retrospect – that they knew a good thing when they saw one.

Racing, to Duke's generation, meant one thing above all others – the

He'd come a long way from those secret races at the local farm, but the Rose of Lancaster still had pride of place on his helmet.
(Maurice Büla)

En route to his fourth title in 1955, old smoothie Duke still made it all look so easy. (Maurice Büla)

Isle of Man. His first race was on the TT course in the 1948 Manx GP, on a production-racer 350 Norton loaned by the factory. This seized after he had run in the top three, but already he had made a strong impression on trackside observers – among them, Norton team boss Joe Craig. He was keeping a keen eye on his new protégé, who would soon bring Norton their only 500 title. Duke was 25, but still a youngster in racing terms; the average age of a grid-full of racers has dropped sharply in modern times.

In 1949, the year Les Graham claimed the first ever World Championship (at the age of 38), Duke, aged 26, won his first TT – the Clubmans, still racing privateer-level Nortons which he prepared himself. He won the Senior class at the Manx GP later in the year. The invitation from Norton followed directly – to join the official factory team for the 1950 season. Duke was on his way – and with a single unexpected honour to start him off. When senior Norton team rider Harold Daniell was injured at the start of the year, it fell to Duke to race the all-new Manx Norton frame for the first time, winning a national race at Blandford almost unopposed. Later that year, the exceptional new chassis would earn the deathless nickname 'Featherbed', and it not only set new standards of comfort and roadholding, but also a fashion for twin-loop frame design that remained an ideal for road and racing bikes for 25 years or more.

At his first attempt, Duke failed to become the second World Champion by only one point. He had won three of the six races, but the crown went to the more consistent two-times winner Umberto Masetti and the Gilera. It might have been very different but for a tyre failure at Spa Francorchamps. Duke, who had won his first Senior TT at record speed three weeks earlier, had a 45-second lead on the penultimate lap when a blow-out forced him to retire.

Duke was setting new standards – visibly so. Having observed how much

Back on a Norton, Duke leads Terry Shepherd and Tom Phillis at the 1959 Ulster GP. (Nick Nicholls)

wind drag was generated by the loose-fitting two-piece leather racing suits of the time, he commissioned a tailored set of form-fitting one-piece leathers, worn with tight boots. He was just a typical champion looking for every advantage he could find; from that time on, racing leathers have followed the pattern he set. Another resolution he made then was to 'consciously make a big effort on the first lap … to demoralise the opposition.' This technique was perfected many years later by Freddie Spencer.

Now 28, Duke was at the peak of his form, and the next year was all his own as his rumbling Norton singles took him to four 500-class wins over the strong Gilera team including Masetti, the AJS pair of Bill Doran and Reg Armstrong, the Moto Guzzis and the new MV Agustas. Not to mention his own factory Norton team-mates. He took his first championship comfortably, adding the 350cc title at the same time, as well as a Senior/Junior TT double that was a source of great pride. As Britain emerged from the hard post-war years with the lavish Festival of Britain, Duke became a national hero. For this was a time of heroes, of dashing test pilots and (two years later) intrepid mountaineers atop Everest, and now there was a debonair motorcycle ace to go with them.

Duke's title defence was successful in the 350cc class in 1952, but his 500 season started badly – the hard-pressed Nortons hit reliability problems in the first two rounds. He was second to Masetti at the next two outings, then Duke made a rare error and crashed at the German GP in the 350 race. He broke his ankle badly, and was out for the rest of what had been a busy year, including four races for the Aston Martin sports car team, finishing second at Goodwood at the first attempt, behind Stirling Moss. Aston Martin were sufficiently impressed to sign him up for 1953 as well, although after driving twice he asked to be released from his contract mid-season.

Motorcycle champion or not, Duke was still a household name, and when news broke at the end of the season that he would be leaving Norton to ride for the Italians, for Gilera, he had some explaining to do. Not that the writing on the wall wasn't obvious. Norton's own four-cylinder racer, to have been developed with a motor design by F1 car firm BRM, was cancelled, and the multi-cylinder machines were clearly faster, even if the light and slender Norton did have better handling. It was a reluctant but necessary move, if he was to challenge for the championship.

Duke and his new Gilera team-mates – Armstrong, Alfredo Milani and Dickie Dale – demonstrated the truth of that most assuredly, as they claimed the first three 1953 championship places ahead of three Nortons, Duke head and shoulders above the rest. He had swept to win after win on the wailing four – out of seven 500-class GPs that year he won four, was second once, and retired in the other two. The following year brought more of the same – five wins, one second place, one retirement. And just to break the pattern in 1955, he won every time he didn't retire, except for one third place. To say he was a regular on the rostrum would rather understate the case.

History threw a shadow over his final title, however, and effectively spoiled any chances of adding a fifth crown in 1956, as after the World Championship he found himself embroiled in a dispute at the Dutch TT in 1955. It concerned starting money for the private riders in the smaller classes. Duke approved their cause, if not their threat of strike action, and

The war of the nations

Which was the most successful nation in the 500 class? Given its dearth of winners over the past 25 years, the rather surprising answer is Great Britain. American riders have won more individual races, but the British more titles – the first statistic might have been different, except that in the early years the championship entailed considerably fewer races.

The sweep of history shows spells – hopefully cycles – of national superiority. British riders claimed 17 out of the 53 crowns available, and all but four of them in the first 20 years. Then it was Italy's turn, with a tranche of 14, well over half of these before 1975 thanks to Agostini's serial success.

Americans have also won 14 titles. The first US rider to win a 500 GP was Pat Hennen in 1976; the first champion was Kenny Roberts in 1978, and from then on they kept rolling on with teams of talent until they finally ran out of riders in the mid-Nineties. A new and last US 500 champion, in 2000, was a full generation down the line – literally, for he was son of the first one.

A decade after the American invasion, a new generation of tough Australians had come to the fore, with one of them – Mick Doohan – achieving almost total domination to win five of the nation's six titles.

One Rhodesian (born in Wales) and one Spaniard make up the élite; by the end of the 500 era the melting pot was brewing again, with America and Italy both resurgent, and a new generation of Japanese stars threatening to build on the inroads already made in the smaller classes.

felt honour-bound to support them, he later explained. As the most prominent member of the group, he also received the greatest punishment imposed by an FIM court at the end of that year – six months suspension starting on 1 January. They relented enough to let him take part in domestic racing to keep his hand in, and he won the final GP of the season, after retiring in the previous three. But having missed the first two rounds completely, he was powerless to prevent the next fast Englishman, John Surtees on the rapidly improving MV Agusta, from ending a highly distinguished reign.

Injury in 1957 spoiled his final year with Gilera, and at the end of that season, in the face of rising costs and falling sales, all the Italian factories agreed to pull out of the GPs, with MV Agusta later changing its mind. Duke returned on a factory BMW, but never did mesh with the shaft-drive twin, and switched back to the faithful Norton for a final win in Sweden. He had one last season as a private entrant, claiming rostrum finishes in the 250, 350 and 500 classes (where he was three times third), and retired at the end of the year.

Duke's car racing career had fizzled out during 1953 – mainly because of friction with the existing drivers, especially Peter Collins, who resented this fast motorcyclist invading his territory; nor was his next racing venture to prosper – an attempt in 1959 to revive the Gileras in a team bearing his own name. Duke didn't care for the taste of losing, but remained as gracious as he had been when winning.

After retirement he moved to the Isle of Man to pursue his business interests, which include hotel development and freight. Although the after-effects of ankle injuries sustained in Germany at the start of his racing career meant he found it difficult to change gear on a motorcycle, preventing more than a handful of demonstration rides in retirement, Duke remains to this day an honoured and respected figure within motorcycling, and especially at the TT.

John Surtees

In 1960, after winning his fourth crown, John Surtees left bikes to conquer car racing. (Nick Nicholls)

It all became 'a bit of a cakewalk'

Surtees tiptoes the MV in the streaming wet. Master of all conditions, he won the first four of the Italian marque's unbeaten eighteen 500-class championships.
(Nick Nicholls)

In his autobiography, John Surtees writes about 'the inherent Surtees family cussedness'. He is describing his father. Many people who knew John as a racer would say the same about him. Certainly he was stubborn. John Surtees was also intelligent, far-sighted, mechanically gifted, intensely competitive, and a perfectionist – qualities that mark out the greatest champions in this and other branches of motorsport. Literally so, in the case of this English rider, who left motorcycling for cars, and four years later won the F1 World Championship in a factory Ferrari. He remains the only two- and four-wheeled World Champion in history.

After retirement, pondering whether two or four wheels had been more important to him, he plumped for motorcycles, writing in *John Surtees – World Champion* (Hazleton): 'The relationship between a rider and a motorcycle is … more personal than that between a driver and his car. On balance … I derived more pleasure from my bike racing career than my time with cars'. This typically painstaking statement will strike a chord with anyone who has ever ridden a motorcycle fast, whether or not they were around when this slightly doleful-looking youngster from the southern outskirts of London emerged at speed in the early Fifties to take over from (to an extent even ousting) the debonair Geoff Duke, discovering new lines, new angles of lean, and new ways of getting speed out of the unwieldy-looking dustbin-faired four-cylinder giants from Italy. Not that John, a cussed Surtees to the core, wouldn't rather have been on a single-cylinder Norton, if only they'd listened to him.

John was the elder of two sons, born on 11 February 1934 in the small village of Tatsfield, on the Kent–Surrey border. His father, Jack Surtees, was a grass-track side-car competitor of note, and it was at the old Brands

Hatch grass-track circuit – local to the South London family – that young John first rode a motorcycle on his own account. It was a Wallis-Blackburne speedway bike, and 13-year-old John ran round and round the cinder access road outside the track. A year later he made an inauspicious competition début, riding passenger in his father's sidecar outfit in a speed trial – they won, but were disqualified because John was under age, but only a year later he was himself racing, grass-tracking on an Excelsior.

Jack was by now in the motorcycle business, trading and repairing bikes in South London, and John was a regular in the workshop, learning basic skills as well as the art of how to get the most out of an existing design or component. Money was tight, but hard work and creative engineering could go a long way to making up for that. And he was racing every weekend – with the stern-faced but invaluable support of his very experienced father, who also had many important contacts in racing and in Britain's then dominant motorcycle manufacturing business. One family friend was the great sidecar champion Eric Oliver.

John started road-racing in 1950, at the new tarmac Brands Hatch, on a Triumph, soon supplemented with a Vincent 500 Grey Flash, on which he claimed his first win. By the age of 17 he had started his apprenticeship at the Vincent works, and they encouraged his racing as he piled success on success on the British short circuits. In 1953, he won 30 out of 60 races entered, but also remembers falling off at almost every race in his early days. Even from the start of his career he found himself up against the hero of the day, Geoff Duke, and a proud press cutting from that time described him as 'the man who made Duke hurry'. The reigning World Champion was to provide a worthy yardstick and target for the fast-rising Surtees.

Surtees and the title-winning MV in 1958. His determination and technical expertise were a big help in taking the factory to dominance.
(Nick Nicholls)

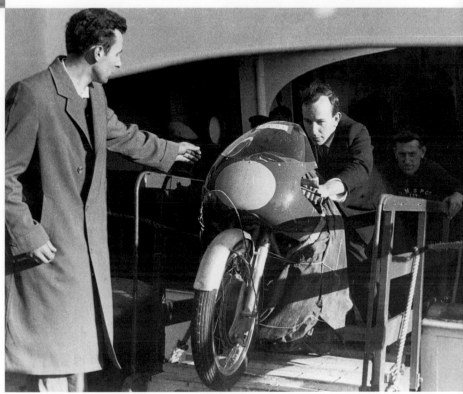

Winners still push. Surtees unloads the MV Agusta off the ferry at the Isle of Man in 1958. He won the race, and the championship.
(Nick Nicholls)

John was first asked to race for the Norton factory at the TT in 1953, but spoiled his chances by crashing a 250 EMC in practice, much to the dismay of legendary team boss Joe Craig. He was good enough to be forgiven, however, and after another strong season in 1954 on his own Nortons he was taken into the factory team in 1955 for 'major events', including a handful of championship rounds. Surtees has a particularly fond memory of his victory over Duke's four-cylinder Gilera in a late-season international at Silverstone in 1955, avenging an earlier defeat at Aintree, and followed by another win at Brands Hatch. This had been a momentous year – Surtees had also ridden a fuel-injected factory BMW during the season, as well as his 250 NSU.

The GP series beckoned for 1956 with several interesting options. Surtees had tentative approaches from Moto Guzzi and Gilera, interest from BMW – although the German factory's plans were indecisive – and a firm offer from MV Agusta to partner Umberto Masetti (*qv*). Most of all he wanted to stay with Norton, where a horizontal-cylinder prototype already offered better performance than the stalwart up-and-down Manx. The pre-eminent racing factory was undergoing major changes, however, including the departure of long-time race boss Craig. Surtees divined correctly that the horizontal Norton would never appear, and decided that the MV Agusta – although in his view inferior to the Gilera – was too good to turn down. And thus was born the first of a series of partnerships that would make the MV name the greatest in racing until Honda took over at the far end of the century.

Unkind observers might remark that Duke's absence from the middle part of the 1956 season after the Assen strike rather helped Surtees to take

Surtees with marque founder Count Domenico Agusta. (Maurice Büla)

By 1960, Surtees was very much the senior British racer. Here he talks to rival John Hartle. (Nick Nicholls)

the title at his first attempt – over Zeller's BMW, and by a big margin – and this has some truth. At the same time, Duke's finishing record was bad when he was there, winning only one race. In any case, winning titles is about beating who is there, and Surtees did this very comprehensively, winning the TT, Assen and Spa before himself suffering a broken arm after falling off the 350 MV at Solitude in Germany to miss the last three races. But for that, he might have taken that title as well.

Gilera took revenge the next year, with the MV four suffering a string of reliability problems, some caused by overheating within the huge 'dustbin' fairings of the day, others (according to Surtees) by sloppy manufacture. The big bodywork was banned for 1958, while in true cussed Surtees style John was putting pressure on the factory to improve the construction of the complex motor. He had little choice but to persevere, since another turn of history had closed down most other options – including the highly interesting prospect of the Guzzi V8, the potential of which had much impressed Surtees when he tested it during 1957. For 1958, Guzzi and the other major Italian factories had pulled out – with the exception of MV.

For the next three years, all Surtees had to do was to beat the other MV riders. This he did with manifest ease, and by the time he got to his third successive title in 1960, which even he described as 'a bit of a cake-walk', it was beginning to pall. Not because he was getting tired of bike racing … quite the reverse. He wasn't getting enough! The MV factory had banned John from taking part in non-championship races on his private machines, and he was restricted to GPs plus a few important international meetings – although these would entail also racing the 350 MV, it wasn't nearly enough

Surtees had a reputation for cussedness – but his force of character was just another winning tool. (Maurice Büla)

Just like before … Surtees is very active in classic revival meetings. He and fellow MV World Champion Phil Read give the fire engines another siren song. (Nick Nicholls)

to keep John happy. (Indeed, the stiffer opposition in the smaller class gave Surtees a better chance to show the strength and depth of his riding, and he won that title as well as the 500 in 1958, 1959 and 1960 to bring his total of titles to seven.) Despairing also at the lack of technical development in the face of a growing threat from Japan, he quit bike racing at the end of 1960.

He hadn't actually planned to retire and said later that he might have been tempted back to bikes in 1962, had an offer come from Honda to develop their four. Instead, he pursued another destiny. In 1959 he'd shown signs of a great gift on four wheels too, having tested Aston Martin sports cars and a Vanwall single-seater. He was urged on by influential supporters inside racing. F1 team owner Ken Tyrrell arranged an F2 car for his first-ever car race in 1960 – he fought and was narrowly beaten by the illustrious Jim Clark. In that same year, while claiming his fourth and final 500-class title, he'd finished second in the British car GP, only his second F1 race, and followed that by crashing out of the lead of his third race. Clearly a natural, he was set on a rapid path via Cooper and Lola to Ferrari from 1963 to mid-1966. He won the World Championship in the red car in 1964 and won admiration not only for his driving and race skills, but also for the galvanising effect he had at Ferrari, and the technical input he brought to the team.

In 1967 the call did come from Honda – but to help with their F1 venture. Surtees claimed the last of his six F1 race wins in two years with

John Surtees and his MV Agusta. The English rider left motorcycles while still dominant, and became the first 500 champion to win a Formula 1 car championship as well, but he never forgot that bikes were his first love.
(Phil Masters)

Honda, before turning to the construction of a machine bearing his own name. Surtees retired from driving at the end of 1972, quitting team ownership also some time later, perhaps worn down by a combination of ill health – the consequence of a heavy crash in a Lola Can-Am sports car in the USA in 1965 – and disillusionment at difficulties not only of finding sponsors but also a driver good enough to satisfy such a hard taskmaster.

In retirement, Surtees has remarried and fathered two daughters. His son Freddie is making his way kart racing. A mellower John Surtees still makes occasional appearances on various classic bikes, including his original Vincent Grey Flash and sundry MV Agustas. It is no cliché to say that he has lost little of the precise skill that made him not only the greatest motorcyclist of his time, but also the greatest all-rounder in motor racing.

Libero Liberati

Born
20 September 1926
Terni, Italy

Died
5 March 1962
Terni, Italy

500cc WORLD CHAMPIONSHIP
1957 – Gilera (Four wins: West German GP, Belgian GP, Ulster GP, Italian GP)

Total 500cc GP wins: 4

A legend in Terni, Libero Liberati won a single crown but interrupted the reign of John Surtees. (Maurice Büla)

This is the most mysterious of all the World Champions. Quiet, thoughtful and retiring, Libero Liberati succeeded once in the Gilera factory's final works-team year, after several years of playing understudy, often the only Italian rider in a team that was home not only to Geoff Duke, but also to other redoubtable foreigners including Bob McIntyre. After that, reportedly resisting invitations to join MV Agusta in the hope that Gilera might return, he dropped from view in international racing.

Liberati – whose name loosely translates as Freedom Freed – continued to race a single-cylinder Gilera Saturno, a long-lived model based on a 500cc road bike, and it was on one of these machines that he met his death in 1962. Practising on a favourite informal open-roads test

The humble man who challenged a Duke

track near his home town of Terni, in the Appennines north of Rome, he lost control while crossing railway lines in wet conditions, and was fatally injured.

Liberati was as popular in Terni as he is little-known outside Italy. It was the local motor club that bought the humble son of a factory worker his first racing motorcycle. Since his death, many legends have grown up around the man who brought glory to the otherwise undistinguished steel-working town. They concern his indomitable spirit, his total love for and dedication to Gilera, and also his enforced period of waiting, when Gilera favoured senior team-mate Duke. It was only after Duke's suspension in 1956 after the Assen incident, runs the legend, that Liberati gained the full access to the four-cylinder machines that he deserved, going on to win the title the next year.

Not everybody shares this view. Contemporary reports describe Liberati's own self-belief compared with Duke's total and obvious mastery as an eccentric delusion, and insist that while naturally Gilera needed to employ the world's greatest riders, if only to prevent them joining rivals

Contemporary reports describe Liberati's self-belief as eccentric.
(Maurice Büla)

The quiet Italian was described as a budding rival to Duke, but his time at the top was to be brief. (Maurice Büla)

Guzzi and latterly MV Agusta, they continued to support Italian riders at the same time, and Liberati was much more a beneficiary than a victim.

Truth is, it doesn't really matter. Libero Liberati's achievement stands in the record books, and he was a worthy and genuine champion who interrupted the reign of John Surtees in a year when he claimed all four of his GP wins. The reverence he excited in Terni sprang out of pride and affection. His death was, of course, a needless tragedy that reinforced the legend.

Liberati began his racing career for Moto Guzzi, but the promising youngster was recruited as a back-up rider for Gilera in 1951, campaigning the Saturno regularly (including occasionally the rare twin-cam variant) in national events, and the four occasionally – notably at Monza for the Italian GP, where he was up to second place before he ran into problems with a broken throttle cable, dropping to seventh.

He continued in this way for the next two years, Duke grabbing most of the wins and the glory for Gilera, and by 1955 was described as 'a budding rival' to Duke, even claiming the odd win over the Englishman in the 350 class in 1956.

Nobody could have said that he was a poor relation in the team in 1957, after the year began with injury to Duke at the prestigious Imola pre-season meeting. This left only Liberati and McIntyre in the team, until Australian Bob Brown was recruited as a last-minute replacement for the TT. By then, Liberati had already beaten McIntyre in Germany, though only narrowly after the Scot made a fine recovery from an early misfire. McIntyre was attempting to defy team orders … that he should finish behind his Italian team-mate.

McIntyre won the TT convincingly, setting the first ever 100mph lap, but at the very next race at Assen he was injured, and effectively out of the championship chase. Liberati was second to Surtees. A week later, Liberati's machine failed to start for the Belgian GP. The team summarily seized Brown's bike for their title hope and Liberati went on to win the race … only to be disqualified for changing bikes without having notified the jury!

One might think that against such a rival as Surtees, losing one race in this way might be enough – but the MV was unreliable in 1957, and Liberati was at the top of his form. This was all demonstrated clearly at the next round, the Ulster GP, where Surtees broke down while leading comfortably until his machine failed, leaving Liberati to a clear and crucial win, with team-mates McIntyre and the returned Duke more than half-a-minute behind. He beat Duke again at Monza for the final race, after Surtees's last-ditch battle for the lead ended as he dropped to fourth with machine trouble. And the crown was his.

The quiet man's time at the top was to be short lived, however. At the end of that season, Gilera announced a withdrawal for the next three years. It turned out to be for rather longer than that, the Duke Gilera team notwithstanding.

Liberati continued to race after the withdrawal of the factory, campaigning among other things a Morini in the 250 class and finishing fourth in Germany on the bike in 1959. The Saturno, however, was outclassed in the 500 class, and he never did score another championship point on a 500.

Gary **Hocking**

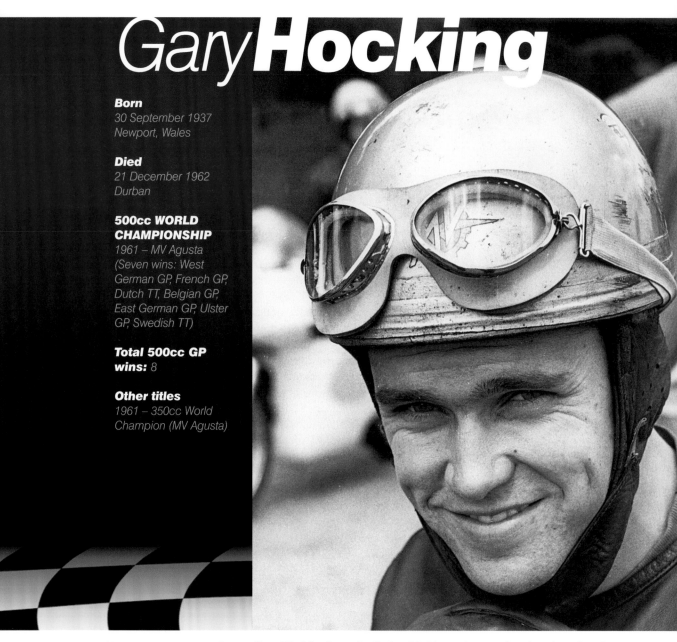

Born
30 September 1937
Newport, Wales

Died
21 December 1962
Durban

500cc WORLD CHAMPIONSHIP
*1961 – MV Agusta
(Seven wins: West
German GP, French GP,
Dutch TT, Belgian GP,
East German GP, Ulster
GP, Swedish TT)*

**Total 500cc GP
wins:** *8*

Other titles
*1961 – 350cc World
Champion (MV Agusta)*

*A lean, independent type, Gary
Hocking is remembered as one of the
all-time great natural talents.*
(Nick Nicholls)

Gary Hocking brought little with him to international racing when he arrived from Rhodesia with barely one year's road racing experience and a suitcase full of dreams. In three years, he did everything, and won everything. Then, as abruptly, he was gone again, turning his back on bikes in disgust at the danger. Less than six months later, 'Sox' was dead.

Those few who knew him, and saw him race, remember him as one of the all-time great natural talents. Jim Redman, compatriot, friend and rival (and the greatest rider never to win a 500 championship) puts him right alongside Hailwood. I was lucky enough to see him myself once, as a teenager in South Africa, and the commitment and speed of his corner entry so impressed that I had my first crash trying to emulate him. I was unlucky enough to be at that same Westmead circuit a year later. My best

Tough colonial with a case full of dreams

friend's father, Dr Dunning, was on medical duty when Hocking overturned a Lotus Formula One car into a gully by the track. He spoke only later about the massive head injuries that killed him.

Now Sox can only be known by his memories.

Redman insists on the spelling, and explains: 'We called him Sox because he didn't like wearing them. He liked those sandals you hooked through your toes. We called them coolie sandals.'

Hocking was something of a Colonial type: lean, tough-looking, taciturn and independent. A sincere, god-fearing man who read the Bible every night, but didn't push it on anyone else, Gary was actually born in Wales, moving with his parents to Southern Rhodesia as a young child. When they later returned home, Hocking was only just a teenager, but he opted to stay on alone, working on the railways and boarding with a Bulawayo family, who had a son of a similar age, Richard Faye. Soon afterwards Faye, a motorcycle racer, was killed while racing near Johannesburg.

Whatever effect the tragedy might have had on Gary, it didn't stop him racing. He hadn't just been bitten by the bug. The phrase is far too mild. Hocking had a talent so great that it propelled him to the front of the field, and drove him on to the highest summit of the sport, at very high speed.

Redman recalls: 'He was very grim and determined. He wanted to win his first race – on a Triumph twin he'd prepared himself. And he would have won it too if something hadn't stopped the bike.'

At the start of his last TT, the Senior in 1962, and taking the fast line round Signpost Corner. Hocking won, but retired abruptly soon afterwards. (Nick Nicholls)

He had some footsteps to follow from what is now Zimbabwe. Not only those of Ray Amm, a Norton star, but the fresh trail blazed by Redman. The two had raced together in Rhodesia and South Africa, and when Redman packed his bags for England in 1958, Gary was struck by how his friend achieved instant success, in the top three in several classes at his first major international meeting at Brands Hatch. 'When he heard what I'd done, he said: "I could have won."' In 1958, Hocking arrived too, at the TT, with (in Redman's phrase) 'a cardboard suitcase containing all his worldly possessions. And it rattled.'

Jim had fixed him a 350 Norton, and a Reg Dearden 500, which he took to a first-time 12th. Impressed, entrant Dearden signed him up pronto. At his next race, the Dutch TT, Hocking was the first single home. By 1959 he was having the odd outing on MZ two-strokes. It serves to underline his impact that he was promptly poached by the MV Agusta factory for 1960, when he finished runner up to his new team-mates – Carlo Ubbiali in the 125 and 250 classes and Surtees in the 350. The talent drove him on. Redman recalls how he had been unbeatable on the dirt tracks in Rhodesia, and likewise in the rain. 'Mike Hailwood said to him once: "You must love the wet." Gary replied: "No. I just don't understand why all the others are so slow. You do the same as you do in the dry, only smoother.'"

Gary's year was 1961. He was the greatest talent on the greatest motorbike. He defeated Franta Stastny's Jawa for the 350 title, and Hailwood (who joined MV for the last race) for the 500 crown. Never mind that his lone MV was streets ahead of the mainly single-cylinder opposition (Hocking won by a full lap in Germany). There was nobody who felt he didn't fully deserve the two crowns.

Apparently, these did not sit easily on his head, however, at a time when the phrase 'racing safety' was a laughable oxymoron, and when the competition was sharpening still further with the encroachment of new and increasingly competitive Japanese factory teams. Plus of course his thrusting new team-mate Mike Hailwood. Redman recalls him saying, early in 1962: "'This is madness. We're all pals – and we're going to kill each other." Every so often, he'd ask me , "don't you ever think about the danger?"'

Hocking raced his MV Agusta in the early internationals, and at the first World Championship round – the Isle of Man TT in June. He and Mike were up against Tom Phillis on the new Honda in the 350 Junior. It was to prove tragic and fateful.

Redman was watching at the foot of Bray Hill. 'Tom Phillis started Number 1 on the Honda; first away. Ten seconds later, Hailwood took off riding Number 3; and another ten seconds Sox, on Number 6. By lap two, it was Sox, Mike and Tom on the road. Gary had a good lead on time. All he had to do was sit there.'

Phillis, chasing hard, crashed at Laurel Bank, a treacherously dark and stony corridor. The Australian rider succumbed to his injuries on the way to hospital. Hailwood beat Hocking, both machines misfiring at the end; Hocking went on to win the Senior brilliantly. But he was distraught. 'I've killed Tom,' he told Redman.

He took part in the Post-TT race at Mallory Park, then travelled directly to the MV factory at Gallarate to meet Count Domenica Agusta. He'd had enough, and seen enough tragedy. He was quitting.

'He offered to repay his fee, but Domenica said: "I respect your decision", and released him from the contract,' said Redman. And this modest, determined, gifted genius left motorcycle racing for good.

He didn't leave racing, however. Buying a second-hand Formula One hack from Tyrrell Formula Junior driver John Love, he performed so well in the four-cylinder car that top-level GP entrant Rob Walker offered him one of the new V8 Lotus-Climax machines for an outing in the season-ending South African races, leading up to the World Championship GP. Hocking was practising at the Westmead circuit outside Durban when the car left the road mysteriously in between two corners.

Redman was also there, and has thought long and hard about the crash. 'I've heard several different explanations. One is that the brakes failed. I know Sox – or me, or Mike, or any of us. If that had happened, he'd have spun the car. Another is that the steering locked up. Then you'd have seen brake marks. He wouldn't have panicked and frozen. Some say he blacked out, from dehydration. I think that was it.

'Sox was staying with me and my wife. We lived nearby at the time. It was blazing hot, but at breakfast he wouldn't drink any juice. He had a theory – that drinking only makes you sweat.'

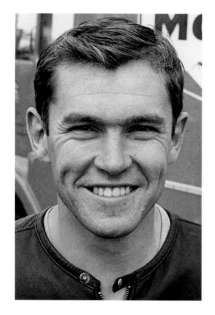

The smile of a private man – few knew Gary Hocking well in his short but brilliant bike racing career.
(Nick Nicholls)

Mike Hailwood

Born
2 April 1940
Great Milton, Birmingham

Died
23 March 1981
Warwickshire

500cc WORLD CHAMPIONSHIPS

1962 – MV Agusta (Five wins: Dutch TT, Belgian GP, Ulster GP, East German GP, Italian GP)

1963 – MV Agusta (Seven wins: Isle of Man TT, Belgian GP, Ulster GP, East German GP, Finnish GP, Italian GP, Argentine GP)

1964 – MV Agusta (Seven wins: US GP, Isle of Man TT, Dutch TT, Belgian GP, West German GP, East German GP, Italian GP)

1965 – MV Agusta (Eight wins: US GP, West German GP, Isle of Man TT, Dutch TT, Belgian GP, East German GP, Czech GP, Italian GP)

Total 500cc GP wins: 37

Other titles

1961 – 250cc World Champion (Honda)

1966 – 250cc World Champion (Honda)
– 350cc World Champion (Honda)

1967 – 250cc World Champion (Honda)
– 350cc World Champion (Honda)

Mike Hailwood seemed to have everything – as a racer and as a man.
(Nick Nicholls)

Genial hero with a giant sense of duty

In the history of motorcycle World Championship racing, Mike Hailwood is the giant. Proof of this, as if it is required, can be found not only in the list of achievements – the titles won, records broken, rivals defeated, motorcycles tamed, and even enemies won over – but in the fact that even in Spain, today the world centre of GP racing, he is still regarded as the greatest ever. When the large-circulation magazine *Motociclismo* ran a readers' poll to mark the first 50 years of the 500 class, the winner was Mike Hailwood – and this is in the fiercely nationalistic home of 13-times 125 champion Angel Nieto.

Mike went on to a high-level career in car racing where, if he stopped short of emulating his predecessor John Surtees, this was attributable to circumstances and injury. After that, he returned to motorcycle racing, to win twice more (at lap record speed) at the Isle of Man, theatre of so many of his past triumphs. It may have been a sentimental journey, but Hailwood always raced to win.

As a racer, Hailwood seemed to have everything – courage, skill, intelligence, tactics, mechanical sympathy, bottomless enthusiasm, and an indomitable spirit. As a person, he added manly looks dominated by an unmistakable chin, and a natural cavalier charm that won him friends and admirers from the lowest to the highest social echelons. Mike was modest and cheerful, in adversity and success alike.

Hailwood's career was punctuated by exceptional acts, and one particularly courageous feat was rewarded with the George Medal, the peacetime VC. It was during his F1 career, when he risked immolation to rescue fellow driver Clay Regazzoni from his blazing BRM. Motorcyclists will have their own stories to offer – one shining example being his ride to victory in the 1965 TT, blood streaking his bold chin and the fairing on his MV Agusta broken after he had crashed and remounted to vanquish team-mate and companion Agostini.

What a bitter irony that this hero of heroes should die so prosaically,

Father and son. Stan Hailwood with Mike and MV teamsters Arturo Magni (left) and Vittorio Carruana. He gave his son the best start in racing. Mike did the rest.
(Nick Nicholls)

Nothing like a nice cup of tea after winning a Senior TT – Hailwood briefs the press in 1961.
(Nick Nicholls)

the innocent victim of a road crash with an illegally U-turning lorry on a dual carriageway near his home. With him in the family Rover, going for a fish and chip supper, were his son David and daughter Michelle. David survived. Michelle was killed instantly and Mike succumbed to his injuries a few days later.

Hailwood began as a shy 17-year-old who might easily have been a figure of fun in the rough-and-ready world of motorcycle racing. Accompanied by his forceful and clearly rather unpopular multi-millionaire father Stan, usually in a splendid special-bodied Bentley Continental, he was a quiet youth. Mike had an enviable fleet of motorcycles at his immediate disposal, tended by professional mechanics and comprehensively replaced and updated as appropriate by Stan, who wielded considerable influence as owner of a nationwide chain of motorcycle shops, Kings of Oxford. Stan would make sure that his son's exploits were fully reported in the contemporary press. In fact, Mike hardly needed any help to get noticed.

Mike had started riding on the family estate, and first raced in 1957. Within two months he had claimed his first win, and by the next year was cutting a swathe through British racing, winning races on everything from 125s to 500s, topping and tailing the season with some holiday racing in South Africa, and forming a strong attachment to the country where he would later live for a few years.

The opportunities to race in Britain at that time, and against first-rate competition, were like those presented to junior US dirt-trackers 20 years later. Hailwood polished his act against Geoff Duke, Phil Read, Derek Minter and other notables. Even now his style was becoming established – sitting well back with his arms out straight, leading with his chin, and looking so relaxed, even in the heat of battle, that he made it all look easy.

Mike had been contesting occasional GPs since 1959, as well as the Isle of Man TT. In 1961, his career as a works rider took off, with a work load that would make a modern rider gasp in disbelief. He joined Honda in the 125 and 250 classes and, later in the year, was head-hunted by MV Agusta for 350 and 500 classes. It was a marvellous year of mixed-discipline success, hallmarked by the first of an eventual total of 14 TT wins, one on each of the Hondas, and his first Senior win on a Norton (MV did not take part). He was the first person ever to win three TTs in a week, and followed it up with the 250 title, the first of three in the class. Just apart from this, he also raced an EMC two-stroke 125, his own Mondial 250, and the faithful 350 and 500 Norton singles, as well as a 350 Ducati, and took part in races in the USA as well. Wins and lap records piled up, as a matter of course, wherever he went.

In 1962 MV Agusta signed him up again for the larger classes, and he campaigned the 125 EMC (something of an MZ clone) and now and then a 250 Benelli single, as well as an MZ at the end of the year. He cruised to his first 500 title, at 22 the youngest rider so far to win it. But with team-mate Hocking retiring mid-season he had to beat only an outclassed bunch of old singles, with Alan Shepherd's Matchless a distant second; Phil Read's Norton even further away in third. Next year was a bit different. The return of the Gileras promised some stiffer opposition, and Mike signed up for MV exclusively, in a 250/350/500 deal. The 250 never did materialise, and Mike was back on the MZ in that class when he claimed another record, the first ever to win three classes at the same GP, at the Sachsenring in East Germany. He clinched a second title, with Shepherd's Matchless again second, the Gilera threat having failed to reach fruition. And he signed up again for a third year with MV Agusta in 1964. That relationship was always somewhat troubled, with the autocratic Count Agusta granting and withholding favours almost wilfully – his policy of only entering races and classes where he was confident of victory also jarred with Mike's race-anything race-anybody philosophy. His third straight 500 title win, again over single-cylinder opposition, came at the same time as his increasing disquiet at not being able to ride the new three-cylinder 350.

Hailwood had already started to race cars, moving straight into Formula One, and driving a Lotus BRM in 1964 with a best finish of sixth in Monaco. The French GP illustrates his busy life. He practised his car in France on Friday, won the 500 GP at Assen on Saturday, raced the car in France on Sunday, and was back on the MV Agusta at Spa Francorchamps the following weekend to win the Belgian GP.

After yet more uncertainty, Mike signed to stay with MV again in 1965. This year would be different. He had opposition – the up-and-coming young Giacomo Agostini was also in the team, and here was someone to beat. Beat him he did, adding eight victories to Ago's maiden win in the class.

Earlier in the year, Mike had temporarily abandoned car racing to devote himself to bikes, and at the end of it his commitment was rewarded with the alliance that would define him more clearly than the easy years at MV Agusta, even though he never was to win another 500cc title. Hailwood had gone back to Honda, with the ever-stronger Japanese company planning a move into 500s with the class heavyweight aboard their bike. He would have old 250/350 rival Jim Redman as his team-mate, and would contest the smaller classes as well.

Hailwood catches the photographer's eye. He went on to win his second 500-class title on the MV in 1963. (Nick Nicholls)

Hailwood and the Honda set off for his epic 1967 TT duel against Agostini's MV. Mike won, Ago broke down. The race is remembered still. (Nick Nicholls)

As it turned out, Redman rode the 500 first, but did not finish the 1967 season after crashing out soon afterwards. Fittingly it was Hailwood who gave Honda their first victory in the class, and he might have won the title too, but for the vicissitudes of a season hit by unpredictable weather. Not to mention that while the six-cylinder 250 Honda was a fine and easy machine, the four-cylinder 500 was an evil-handling brute capable of wiping the smile off even Hailwood's face. He won both 250 and 350 titles, but Ago won the 500.

The timing was bad. At the same time, Honda had also moved into Formula One, a venture that precipitated a financial crisis. In 1968, they cut back on their bike programme, supporting only the larger classes, though they did enlarge the six to 350cc to help Mike claim a second crown in that category, along with another 250 title. But the 500 was plagued with ill handling and an unreliable gearbox, and though Mike added five more race wins to equal Agostini's tally for the year, on secondary results the Italian had the advantage once again. Honda's – and Hailwood's – attempt had failed.

And that was more or less that, for racing's brightest star, at least as far as GP motorcycle racing was concerned. Especially since Honda made it financially worth his while not to race any other makes in World Championship events, lending him a 250 and a 500 for his own use. MV tried to entice him back for 1969, but Hailwood told his then interviewer and now biographer Mick Woollett: 'It's the terrific strain of responsibility that has robbed racing of most of its pleasure for me … You go to a meeting knowing everyone from your bosses down to the youngest spectator is expecting you to win.' The evil handling of the big Honda had also left him disturbed – his own experiments with privately commissioned frames having been quashed by Honda.

Mike didn't quit bike racing for two more years, racing at Daytona in 1970 and 1971, with a couple of other appearances in the second year. But he was getting serious about cars now, racing sports cars and F5000 from 1969, joining Team Surtees in 1971, and jousting for the lead in the F1 GP at Monza, eventually finishing a close fourth. In 1972 he was European Formula Two champion, in 1973 he suffered from machine unreliability in the Surtees, but moved up to the Yardley McLaren team in 1974 – only to have his season and ultimately his career cut short by serious leg injuries in a crash at the old Nürburgring.

Mike the Bike hadn't finished yet. Now married to Pauline, he moved for a while to South Africa before settling in New Zealand. Then, stung by the criticism of the TT circuit, and its loss of World Championship status, he planned a come-back to the TT in 1978. It was to be historic and uplifting. Riding a big V-twin Ducati Mike won the F1 TT, with a record speed. But his attempt to win the Senior on a 500 Yamaha was unsuccessful, leaving Hailwood with a feeling of unfinished business. After a few more outings in 1978, he returned to the Island in 1979, and added another record lap and a final Senior TT win riding a Suzuki.

It was a fitting punctuation for a legend. Mike now retired and, but for the criminal negligence of a truck driver on a wet evening in late March, would surely still now be a well-loved figure, the personification of sportsmanship and excellence. Instead he is a motorcycle racing icon, who will never be forgotten.

These boots are made for racing. France, 1967. (Maurice Büla)

Giacomo *Agostini*

Born
16 June 1942
Brescia, Italy

500cc WORLD CHAMPIONSHIPS

1966 – MV Agusta (Three wins: Belgian GP, Finnish GP, Italian GP)

1967 – MV Agusta (Five wins: West German GP, Belgian GP, East German GP, Finnish GP, Italian GP)

1968 – MV Agusta (Ten wins: West German GP, Spanish GP, Isle of Man TT, Dutch TT, Belgian GP, East German GP, Czechoslovakian GP, Finnish GP, Ulster GP, Italian GP)

1969 – MV Agusta (Ten wins: Spanish GP, West German GP, French GP, Isle of Man TT, Dutch TT, Belgian GP, East German GP, Czechoslovakian GP, Finnish GP, Ulster GP)

1970 – MV Agusta (Ten wins: West German GP, French GP, Yugoslav GP, Isle of Man TT, Dutch TT, Belgian GP, East German GP, Finnish GP, Ulster GP, Italian GP)

Matinee idol looks and a deep well of stylish riding talent made Giacomo Agostini a natural star. (Nick Nicholls)

Giacomo Agostini's record in the 500 class is unmatched. Eight championships, seven of them in consecutive years; 68 GP wins (beaten only by Doohan, who had the advantage of several more races each year). And, just to crown it all, he was the first person ever to win the 500 title on a two-stroke.

Given this distinction, it is perhaps inevitable that some people like to point out that Ago achieved his success against little or no opposition. For heaven's sake, Ago was wont to win races by a whole lap, on occasion. And when Phil Read joined the MV team, suddenly he was coming second.

This point of view is ignoble and unfair, ignoring as it does not only that Ago had a highly successful 350 career with seven crowns in that class as well, that among the 500-class rivals he defeated was Mike Hailwood on the four-cylinder Honda, that he won no less than ten times at the cruel and punishing Isle of Man TT, and that – most crucially of all – his turning-point two-stroke title was achieved over a season of bitter contest.

Giacomo himself remained aloof from this sort of controversy. His image was always that of a dashing but gentlemanly figure whose oft-quoted 'film-star good looks' had a touch of hauteur. He lived the part – he always knew how to be the right kind of hero.

Like Hailwood, Agostini came from a privileged and wealthy background: his family fortune came from ownership of the ferry company plying across Lake d'Iseo, near the family home in Brescia. Here the parallel ends, for Agostini had no helpful and partisan paternal backing in his road-racing career. Rather the reverse; his family had encouraged youthful fun on play bikes, but did everything they could to stop the young 'Mino' (from the diminutive Giacomino) from going road racing.

Mino had his first motor scooter at nine. Two years later he was riding in gymkhanas, and by 15 in trials. It was a short step to the tarmac, and in his late teens he was competing at hill climbs and in junior championships. Family opposition obliged him to secrecy at this stage.

Driven by the potent combination of talent and desire, and rewarded by early success and recognition, Ago could hardly keep the secret for long: at the age of 20 he had won his first national championship, riding a 175cc Morini. Talent-spotted by the Morini factory, he made his GP début in 1964, taking fourth place in the Italian GP and winning the national 250 title. Ago was on the fast track to the top.

The next year, he got there – signed by the all-dominant MV Agusta team to race alongside Mike Hailwood, as apprentice to the master. Ago had never raced anything bigger than a 250. He finished second that year, usually a long way behind – though in the final round at Monza he was just 11 seconds adrift. On the 350 – where he was shown Italian favour when given the new and lighter three-cylinder model before his illustrious team-mate – he not only outpointed Mike, but just missed the World Championship (to Redman's Honda) because of a breakdown in the final race. Two weeks before Monza, Ago had claimed his first 500 win in Finland, in newly-confirmed champion Hailwood's absence.

In the second year, Ago's apprenticeship was over – and his teacher gone. Hailwood had moved to Honda and was the competition. The big four Honda – clumsy though it may have been – was a new serious rival to

Opposed or alone, Ago was the biggest winner

the MVs as well, after the departure of the other Italian teams. They responded with a development of their lighter and more wieldy 350 triple, first expanded to 420cc, later to the full 500.

Once Hailwood had got the politics and teething troubles out of the way, it was a battle of the titans, won by Agostini. Among a number of vicissitudes for both riders, there hadn't been any close races, however. These were reserved for the 350 class, where Hailwood emerged triumphant. But in the senior class, Agostini had deposed the king. A new order had emerged.

Then came 1967, and Hailwood's chance for revenge, on a more mature motorcycle. The fact that Ago emerged triumphant was the achievement which really underlined the stature that for many years after this one would remain unchallenged.

There were ten races. At the first, at the Hockenheimring, Ago was a full 30 seconds adrift when the leading Honda's crankshaft broke. He inherited the win.

The next confrontation came on the Isle of Man, and those who saw it will never forget an epic TT, perhaps the best ever. The advantage went back and forth as they circulated within seconds of one another against the clock. Ago led, Mike pulled him in, then lost the lead again in a long pit stop to fix a loose twist-grip. Riding superbly Hailwood closed in on the Agusta once again on the final lap – but Ago responded, and was ahead once more on the run over the mountain, by two slender seconds. Then – disaster. His chain broke. Hailwood – fighting with the still-loose throttle – was the winner; both were heroes.

They did the double act again at Assen, Hailwood winning by just over

New kid on the MV team – Agostini cuts a fine figure in 1965.
(Maurice Büla)

MV Agusta's three-cylinder 500 was all but unbeatable in the hands of Agostini. This is in 1966, his first championship year. (Nick Nicholls)

five seconds after 20 laps in close company. One week later, Ago outpaced the Honda at the fast Spa circuit. Each had won two races so far.

At the Sachsenring in East Germany, Ago made it three, taking the points lead for the first time as the defeated Hailwood eventually retired with gearbox problems. A week later, Hailwood claimed victory by almost 20 seconds at Brno, keeping the battle alive with four races remaining.

Rain in Finland saw Hailwood slide off while leading, handing Ago another win – but it wasn't over yet. The Ulster GP, at Dundrod, was a Hailwood/Honda triumph, Agostini out of the points with clutch trouble. Two rounds to go, just six points in it. But the mathematics were not so simple, with only the best six results counting that year. Monza came next, and it was a crucial race. Round the historic wooded parkland Hailwood pulled steadily away to a seemingly unassailable lead. Then he started to slow, and the crowd went wild as Ago and the MV started to reel him in. Mike had gearbox trouble again, and Ago took the lead with one of the 35 laps still to go. In the end, this clinched the title for he needed to finish only second at the final one-off Canadian GP, and this he duly did.

For the next few years, it was all downhill for Ago – in the sense of it being something of an easy free-wheeling cruise. In 1968, with Hailwood and the Japanese rivals gone, he won and took fastest lap at all 10 rounds. His nearest rival was Jack Findlay, riding Norton or Matchless. Often as not, privateer Jack was the only rider still on the same lap as Ago.

The next year, he won the first ten of 12 races, five of them by a full lap. And again in 1970, and the first eight in 1971. This year, there was a harbinger – his closest rival was Keith Turner from New Zealand – riding a

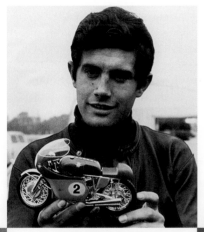

Honey, they shrunk the bike: Ago toys with the MV in 1967.
(Nick Nicholls)

Ago, alone and unopposed in Ulster in 1968 – all year he raced on, even though there was nobody there to race. (Nick Nicholls)

two-stroke Suzuki. The world of racing was beginning to change. So too was the old order at MV. Founder Count Domenico Agusta died in 1971, and his son Corrado took over the title and the factory.

In 1972 Ago kept on winning. But the challenge from the two-strokes was growing – in the 350 class, and now even in the 500 class, with a crop of oversized '351' Yamahas beginning to prove a serious nuisance at the slower circuits.

Agostini had never lost his dignity during the easy years. He always rode fast and flawlessly, with impeccable style. If there'd been anyone to push him, he certainly looked ready to respond. Perhaps he grew complacent. Winning every race you start must inevitably have that effect. But now the Agusta citadel was under serious siege. Over the coming years Ago would have another chance to show the full depth of his ability.

For 1972, MV had enlisted the help of some new team-mates – Alberto Pagani on the 500, who was a clear but usually distant second; and more significantly a really fast man to help Ago win the 350 crown. They hired Phil Read – on the rebound from Yamaha.

Read was a different calibre of companion. Already champion in the smaller classes, and hungry for more, the Englishman came to the Italian team with the firm belief that the end justified the means. For Ago, it was the start of a nightmare. Although he won the 350 title once again in 1973, Read dutifully playing his support role, he was outmanoeuvred in the boardroom, and was obliged to watch – and to consider the value of all

In 1969, Agostini was everybody's target. He kept cool, and generally kept the three-cylinder MV comfortably in front. (Nick Nicholls)

Still dominant in 1970, Agostini races the three-cylinder MV at Brands Hatch. (Nick Nicholls)

those years of loyal service – as the new guy got the new bike in the 500 class: a four that outdated his now-aging triple.

There was a reason for this: Ago had a dreadful start to the year in the big class. He crashed in France chasing Jarno Saarinen's Yamaha, a full factory four-cylinder machine, and broke down in Austria and Germany. He didn't score a point until he finally won at Belgium, the seventh round. By then, Saarinen was dead, and Read had already chalked up two wins. Ago fought to the end to retain his crown – but it finally went to his hated team-mate. Agostini was desolate.

His response was drastic. He changed sides, joining Yamaha in a late signing for 1974, to ride their new monoshock in-line four-cylinder 500, updating the previous year's most serious two-stroke challenger yet. Agostini was leading the first race at Clermont Ferrand in France when he retired with gearbox failure; at Imola he ran out of fuel while leading Franco Bonera's MV; but by then he had already won in Austria, and would do so again at Assen, his team-mate Tepi Lansivuori pushing Read's MV to third. Read ran away to win the next weekend at Spa, then the fight was over. Agostini collided with Barry Sheene's new Suzuki when it seized in Sweden, and broke his shoulder. From then on, Read and Bonera moved ahead unhindered, first and second overall for MV's last ever title.

Read put up a spirited defence in 1975, but Agostini and the Yamahas were unstoppable. Agostini won the first round in France, team-mate Hideo Kanaya dutifully half a second behind; Kanaya won in Austria after

By 1973, the two-strokes and some fast new riders were threatening the MV dominance. Here, young Barry Sheene on a Suzuki chases Ago at a non-championship meeting.
(Nick Nicholls)

Sweden, 1975. On the dirt, on the edge, on the title-winning Yamaha – he didn't finish the race, but went on to take the first-ever two-stroke 500cc title. (Henk Keulemans)

Agostini's motor seized, then the Italian went on to win again at the Hockenheimring and at Imola. And almost at Assen – he and Sheene crossed the line side by side, credited with the same finishing time, but the race was given to the Suzuki rider. Read's MV was almost 50 seconds behind in third. Another seize and a flat tyre ruled Ago out in Belgium and Sweden, but a win in Finland and second (to Read) at Brno were enough for him to reclaim his crown. And to stand at the cornerstone of history.

After this achievement, an element of theatre entered his career. For 1976 he rejoined MV Agusta, for instance, winning one final race for the marque at the old Nürburgring. It was also his own last win, bringing his total to 68 – just one of many records he established. Not even Mick Doohan's 54 wins come close, and Agostini's record can now never be challenged.

Later that year he switched to a private Suzuki, and had some undistinguished outings in 1977, but for a second place at Hockenheim on a quirky three-cylinder 350 Yamaha built unofficially in Holland, behind his identically-mounted team-mate, the eventual champion Takazumi Katayama. At the end of that year he retired.

Ago went on to a distinguished career as manager of the factory Yamaha team, enjoying Marlboro backing, and a run of success that started with Kenny Roberts Senior and went on until 1984, with Eddie Lawson.

In the end, Ago was rather swept aside by modern racing: his Yamaha team and Marlboro sponsorship hijacked by a combination of circumstances and thrusting ex-rider Kenny Roberts, by now well into his own maverick career as team owner. He returned again with Lawson, as head of the Cagiva team, but this was increasingly a figurehead role, for Agostini – now finally married after enjoying many years as one of the world's more eligible bachelors – was beginning to prefer the life of semi-retired gentleman and respected former multiple champion.

And one of racing's all-time greatest.

Here in his final season he is on the two-stroke Yamaha at the 1977 British GP. (Nick Nicholls)

Concentrating (Maurice Büla), *and full of fun.* (Nick Nicholls)

Phil Read

Born
1 January 1939
Luton, Bedfordshire,
England

500cc WORLD CHAMPIONSHIPS
1973 – MV Agusta (Four
wins: West Germany,
Dutch TT, Swedish GP,
Spanish GP)

1974 – MV Agusta (Four
wins: French GP, Belgian
GP, Finnish GP, Czech GP)

Total 500cc GP wins: 11

Other titles
1964 – 250cc World
Champion (Yamaha)

1965 – 250cc World
Champion (Yamaha)

1968 – 125cc World
Champion (Yamaha)
– 250cc World
Champion (Yamaha)

1971 – 250cc World
Champion (Yamaha)

1977 – TT Formula One
World Champion (Honda)

Phil Read, who enjoyed the nickname 'Rebel Read', had a highly successful career, with controversy following him all the way. (Nick Nicholls)

One might say there are two types of champion in this book. There are the old-style racers, generally aged in their 30s, racing two or three classes a day, over much longer distances although at fewer events, and meeting also at big-money international meetings. Then there are the moderns, a new generation of younger, highly-specialised big-bucks superstars, taking part only in GPs, where they sprint-race fearsomely overpowered brutes for 40 giddy minutes.

Phil Read is both of those types. His career, the longest of any of the 500 champions, spans each era, and he was highly successful throughout, winning World Championship races on everything from single-cylinder Nortons to four-cylinder MV Agustas; from two-cylinder production-racing Yamahas to factory V4 racers, from four-strokes to two-strokes, from

Had longest career but felt he never belonged

tiddlers to monsters. He won GPs in all four classes – 125, 250, 350 and 500 – and the World Championship in all but the 350 class (a feat matched in 2001 by Valentino Rossi). Then a final title, almost after retirement, in the short-lived TT Formula One class, to bring his total to eight.

Typically, perhaps – for he enjoyed and lived up to the nickname 'Rebel Read' – he did it all rather the wrong way round. Riding for Yamaha, Read had been highly influential in the two-stroke revolution. But when it started to take hold in the 500 class, he switched to four-strokes to fight MV Agusta's final defence. Single-minded as ever, he effectively ousted Agostini from MV, beating him twice to claim the last-ever four-stroke title.

Read had a clarity of purpose that made enemies, because he failed to conceal the uncomfortable truth – that winning wasn't only about being faster on the bike. It also involved defeating other people – including team-mates. Ago was not the first to feel the cold wind. Six years earlier, Read and Yamaha team-mate Bill Ivy had a spectacular grudge match, with Ivy coming off the worse. Phil Read really was the team-mate from hell.

Read, an only child brought up by his mother, was always solitary. Motorbikes ran in the family – his mother rode well into her seventies – and Phillip William Read bought his first bike, a pre-war 250 Matchless, with Christmas present money, at the age of 13. The family property had space, including a tennis court and adjoining banks, where he could scramble and slide and race against the stopwatch with his friends, and he also taught himself technical understanding of the machine.

How does the racing bug find its victims? Read was one among many inspired by watching the exchange of the torch between Duke and Surtees.

The man who ousted Agostini, Read won his first title, and MV Agusta's 17th rider's crown, in 1973. (Maurice Büla)

Emulating them on the roads was fun, but frightening and dangerous. In 1956, at the age of 17, Read went racing to be safer.

Now serving an engineering apprenticeship in his home town of Luton, north of London, Read bought a BSA Gold Star which he would ride to British circuits, strip of its road fittings, and then race. Talent, as it will, showed early. So too did the badger-striped helmet, inspired by Guzzi star Bill Lomas, and still then in Luton Town football colours rather than his trade-mark white on black.

Fettling the Goldie in a paddock somewhere, Read would watch a contemporary rookie in some amazement. Mike Hailwood used to arrive chauffeur-driven in his father's Bentley, with a fleet of bikes to race in several classes. Worse still, he was so fast. Mike was to be counterpoint to Read as both scaled the heights of racing – an inspiration and a bête noire. As Phil memorably said: 'If Mike hadn't been such a great guy, it would have been really easy to dislike him.'

By 1958 Read had bought a 350 Manx Norton, making a Manx GP début and racing all over Britain. Hailwood was the golden boy, and in 1959 Read finished second to him in the 350 and 500 ACU Star national championships. But it was Read who won the Manx GP, having acquired his first 500cc Norton, and at the end of 1960, as Hailwood's shining path took him to MV and Honda and the start of the glory years, Read finished his engineering apprenticeship and threw in his job. At the age of 21, he was a professional racer.

He spent the next years putting himself on the map, making his full TT début in 1961 with an important first-year Junior TT win, as well as moving abroad to Assen and Spa Francorchamps, finishing the year with a

The smile of a tiger – Read was a challenging team-mate as well as rival, and the ends justified the means. (Nick Nicholls)

Read claimed the last-ever four-stroke title on the MV in 1974. (Nick Nicholls)

successful South African tour. More of the same in 1962 saw Read an unexpected if rather distant third in the 500 championship to winner Hailwood and second-placed Alan Shepherd. Phil had only taken part in two of that year's eight races.

By now seriously in demand, Read was snatched away from top Norton tuner Steve Lancefield for Geoff Duke's high-profile 1963 attempt to revive the four-cylinder Gileras, replacing the injured Derek Minter. It was not a happy partnership. The obsolescent Gilera gave Read his 'most frightening TT ever' as it weaved and veered from bump to bump in his vain chase of eventual champion and race winner Hailwood's MV Agusta. Revealingly, he later wrote in *Phil Read: The Real Story* (MacDonald & Jane): 'I never really felt I belonged,' which might stand as something of a mantra for this independent rider. Duke's comments were also frank. Read, he said, had 'exceptional ability,' but 'was an individualist, not a team man … incapable of accepting advice from any quarter, no matter how well intentioned or informed.'

Others concentrated on the exceptional ability. Before the end of 1963 came the telegram from Japan, inviting Read to join Yamaha, who had built a new four-cylinder 250 after a first unsuccessful attempt to go racing. Read would be the focus of the team, as it embarked on a fine technical adventure.

Read's Yamaha years were the best of his career, and he gave a foretaste in his first ride on the two-stroke at the end-of-season Japanese GP of 1963, in a wheel-to-wheel heart-in-the-mouth duel with Jim Redman's 250 Honda. The Yamaha faltered before the finish, but this double-act was to run and run. 'The 250 class became the race to see,' said Read. He claimed his first GP win in France and spent the year battling with Redman, prevailing in the end by just four points.

Read swept to a second successive title the next year, and team-mate Mike Duff also outpointed a troubled Redman, now riding the exotic six-

Concentration was the name of the game. Mallory Park, 1975.
(Nick Nicholls)

It's not a GP, and Sheene (7) is on a 750 Suzuki two-stroke against Read's 500 MV. But the omens are clear enough. (Nick Nicholls)

cylinder Honda. Read added TT wins, lap records and pole positions, but in 1966 Hailwood joined Honda, and with the six now well-tamed he seemed to find it easy to deny his old rival a third 250 title in succession. Another significant entry – British racer Bill Ivy, short and stocky and staggeringly competitive – was Read's new Yamaha team-mate. They were friends for as long as two such fierce rivals can be, perhaps longer, for in 1967 the pair remained more than cordial as Ivy won the 125 title, and Read tied on points in the 250 with Hailwood, who was awarded the title after a controversial FIM decision.

Then it all blew up: 1968 was the year of the great Read/Ivy feud – the year 'Rebel Read' went public. Honda had unexpectedly withdrawn from racing, Yamaha had the 250 and 125 classes to themselves, and they decided that Read should win the smaller class, but the 250 crown was earmarked for Ivy. Read chafed under these team orders, then – before the year was over – divined that Yamaha were probably also going to quit at the end of 1969. Therefore this might be his last chance at the 250 title. At the Czech GP, he decided that he was going to race to win both titles. The 125 crown was safe; he and an angry Ivy tied for points in the 250, and this time, aggregate race times gave the crown to Read.

Ivy classed Read as a traitor, and bitterly turned his back on motorcycles to embark on a promising four-wheel career. Then he came back to race the 250 Jawa but, in practice in East Germany, crashed fatally when it seized on a wet track. Read had only one regret – that Ivy died before he'd had a chance at least to explain himself: 'I gained the title but lost a friend.'

Yamaha did pull out, and Read found himself racing as a privateer again in 1969, on a pair of production Yamahas, mainly in Britain – although he did claim a 250/350 double at the Italian GP, two tenths ahead of Kel Carruthers, whose Benelli that year won the last-ever four-stroke 250 title.

The MV on song in 1975, Read's last year on the bike. (Nick Nicholls)

Read had another landmark in sight now – to become the first privateer ever to win the 250cc Championship. Working alone in 1971, riding a Helmut Fath-tuned Yamaha, Read claimed three early-season wins to defeat Yamaha factory-backed defender Rod Gould by five points. The rebel had scored again.

Now 32 years old, Read had a superb all-rounder career behind him, and a string of titles. He was a willing superstar with a glamorous lifestyle: the tow-car for his paddock caravan was a Rolls-Royce; he also bought a light aircraft and a fair copy of a manor house in the heart of the Surrey stockbroker belt. Some riders would have been satisfied. But this book is about 500 champions, and they are made of hungrier stuff.

Read spent another two years riding private Yamahas, but in the second he embarked on yet another facet of his career. He'd been signed up by MV Agusta, to support Agostini in the 350 class, and in 1973, he'd moved up into the factory's 500 team alongside his old Italian rival.

After Ivy's experiences, Ago may well have had misgivings. They were well-founded. Before long Read was riding the new four-cylinder MV while Ago languished on the older triple, compounding his bad start to the 1973 season. MV's strongest rival, Yamaha's genius Jarno Saarinen, was killed in a race crash in the third round at Monza. By the end, Read had added a first 500-class title to his collection. In 1974, Ago left MV Agusta after nine years and seven titles; the presence of Read had made his position untenable.

The two were head-to-head for the next two years, Read defending the faith on the MV, Ago now heading Yamaha's two-stroke challenge. Read won the first encounter, claiming the last-ever four-stroke title on the MV again in 1974; next year Ago took the first two-stroke title. It was the changing of the guard.

For 1976 Read bought himself a square-four Suzuki two-stroke to try to repeat his privateer success in the top class. The challenge didn't last long. By the sixth round in Belgium, lagging on points after factory Suzuki star Barry Sheene's four wins, Read suddenly found himself overcome with disillusionment and ennui. The kid was running away with it, and suddenly the game wasn't worth the candle. Read jumped into his Rolls-Royce and drove home without even waiting for the race. Soon afterwards, he announced his Grand Prix retirement.

Read raced at non-championship meetings for the rest of that year, gave the MV a couple of last sentimental outings, and raced now and then for Honda Britain. But this enigmatic man had one last card to play, and one last World Championship to win. At, of all places, the Isle of Man.

Read's relationship with the Island had been (what else?) controversial. Six times winner, he had also been a leading critic of the dangerous track's inclusion as a championship round. The race was stripped of that status for 1977, and given a special TT F1 'World Championship' of its own. Who returned to win it? None other than Phil Read – demonstrating, if nothing else, that he wasn't personally too scared to race round the Mountain Circuit.

After retirement, neither Read's personal life nor his business enterprises prospered. But he retained a keen interest in racing, with a penchant for alternative technologies that might one day achieve his dream of seeing a British machine back at the top of racing.

Phil Read was the last of five riders to win the 500cc title on the MV Agusta.
(Phil Masters)

Barry*Sheene*

Born
11 September 1950
Holborn, London,
England

500cc WORLD
CHAMPIONSHIPS
1976 – Suzuki (Five wins:
French GP, Austrian GP,
Italian GP, Dutch TT,
Swedish GP)

1977 – Suzuki (Six wins:
Venezuelan GP, West
German GP, Italian GP,
French GP, Belgian GP,
Swedish GP)

Total 500cc GP
wins: *19*

Barry Sheene pointed the way to a new
professionalism, with his combination
of riding ability, ambition, intelligence
and vision. (Henk Keulemans)

Barry Sheene was the greatest all-rounder of the lot. This bold
statement isn't made because of the range of his motorcycling
accomplishments, for he concentrated almost exclusively on modern
short-circuit road-racing, but because of the overall breadth of his
talents. He had very many of them, all of which he put to full use, and
they reached far beyond the necessary ability to understand motorcycles
and how to ride them fast, far beyond racing itself. Sheene's great
strengths included riding ability, ambition, intelligence and vision.
Deployed in that order, they made him formidable. No rider before him
had ever seen the big picture quite as clearly.

One example can be found in the voluminous press coverage he
generated. It helped to put motorcycle racing into the limelight in a new

Gifted all-rounder who saw the big picture

world driven by the media – especially television – and big-money sponsorship. Until now, by and large, if riders had seen the value of press coverage, it was primarily to psyche out their rivals. Barry spoke not only to the other racers, but also directly to every reader and every TV viewer. He played the media to charm the public. And because he backed up that charm with the most admirable and conspicuous sort of personal courage, it made him even greater.

He showed his mettle in the way he fought back from injury after two serious high-speed crashes – the first, alone, on the Daytona banking at 170mph in 1975, the second in 1982 at Silverstone, in a collision not a great deal slower. The injuries, and the indomitable way Barry dealt with them, made him seem more human and all the more beguiling. Even in adversity, he seemed to lead a charmed life, and in this way, he achieved unprecedented fame, and diverted unprecedented amounts of money into his bank accounts. Oh, and won two consecutive World Championships in the process.

In a way, the titles do seem almost incidental – because to British fans Sheene was a champion long before that 1976–77 double, and remained champion even in defeat for many years afterwards. He was just as good at being a celebrity as at cracking the throttle open, and perhaps even better. Sheene is remembered more as the cheeky cheery Cockney in the Brut aftershave advertisements or the Texaco posters, and as the dolly-boy racer who ran off with (and later married) a society fashion photographer's wife than as he is for being double World Champion.

Which rather misses the point, because Sheene was a skilful and

Sheene's star was rising in 1975, and his Suzuki links just beginning. (Phil Masters)

Where champions learned how: Barry Sheene (2) in the thick of a 1973 pack of top British riders. Stan Woods leads; Percy Tait (8) and Dave Croxford (4) are the young future champion's tutors for the afternoon at Mallory Park's high-level Post-TT race. (Phil Masters)

smooth racer, an artful exponent of the outer edges of tyre adhesion, a master of wet conditions, and a brave competitor always. His two championship may have looked easy, but he did everything required of a champion: he was the best man on the best bike, and he beat everyone else who was there. And he was on the top bike because he made sure of it, employing his full range of personal resources and not a little cunning to secure the pick of the latest factory parts for his Suzuki. Another team-mate from hell? For some, yes. But what a charmer with it.

Barry, younger brother to Maggie, was born in Gray's Inn Road, London, and grew up not quite a Cockney, in a flat at the examination halls of the Royal College of Surgeons, where his father Frank was the chief engineer. Frank was also a former rider and now a noted private entrant and tuner in England, particularly with the two-stroke Bultacos from Spain. Barry was tinkering and riding from early boyhood. His first track appearance was as a junior hack, running in the brand-new 125 and 250 Bultacos of 1968. Brands Hatch observers noted that the kid was smooth, consistent, and notably fast. It was a short step to club racing and then national competition, with Barry cutting a swathe on his 125cc Bultaco. Given his family connections, they were good bikes. He rode them well, he tuned them to go better. He could think. And he was hard to beat, winning the national 125 championship in 1970.

That was on an ex-factory Suzuki, the factory having withdrawn from racing temporarily. It was an astute purchase and the key to his World Championship début in 1971, when he also rode a 50cc Kreidler, a 250cc Derbi, and 250 and 350cc Yamahas. This was some start. Barry won two of

By the seventh of ten rounds, in Sweden, Sheene needed only one more victory to secure the title. He took it. (Henk Keulemans)

Sheene won the first GP of 1976, the French. (Henk Keulemans)

the 125 GPs and chased Angel Nieto all the way to the finish for the title, adding a 50cc win just for good measure.

If 1972 was a down year on a pair of very temperamental factory 250 and 350 Yamahas, which Sheene complained about with some enthusiasm, 1973 was the opposite. Sheene joined Suzuki, a defining partnership. This gave him two theatres of war. Aboard the three-cylinder 750 he was invincible, sweeping to victory in his national and the FIM's international F750 championships. On his other bike, a 500, he also won the British title in that class, as well as becoming King of Brands. In the annual readers' poll run by the popular weekly *Motor Cycle News*, he was voted *MCN* Man of the Year, an award he would win five times in eight years. Sheene shone, and could do no wrong.

Sheene's first Suzuki 500 was a primitive air-cooled hybrid, based on a road-going twin in a racing chassis. His class début, in Finland, ended in a non-finish. But Suzuki had something special in the pipeline – the new RG500 square four. It was nothing but the cleverest-yet 500cc two-stroke, which would go on to claim seven consecutive manufacturers' titles, and still be winning riders' titles right up until 1982.

Sheene gave the new bike its maiden outing in 1974, and if it was not yet very reliable, he was on the rostrum in two out of three finishes. The next year began with near disaster – the well-publicised 170mph crash, captured on film, when a rear tyre burst at full speed on the Daytona banking. The worst of multiple injuries was a broken femur, and the subsequent pinning and bolting operations were widely reported, as was Barry's notably determined quick recovery. He was still too late to prevent Agostini taking the first-ever two-stroke 500 title, although he

Sheene won his first 500 GP at Assen in 1975. Here, one year later, he came back to do it again – and went on to his first championship. (Henk Keulemans)

Sheene's Suzuki team-mate in 1976 and 1977 was American Pat Hennen – first American to win a 500 GP, but just another rider for the Briton to beat. (Henk Keulemans)

did win both the GPs that he finished.

The stage was set now for two years of domination, with the Suzuki both well-polished and reliable. Fortuitously, Agostini and later Read dropped out of the picture. With Cecotto failing to perform on the Yamaha, Sheene's closest opposition came from other Suzuki riders, including his new team-mate, fast Californian rookie Pat Hennen. He trounced them magnificently, and so easily that he didn't even bother to attend the last three rounds, at the dangerous old-style circuits at Imatra, Brno and the Nürburgring. He had won every other race he'd started (missing also the Isle of Man TT), except the Belgian GP, where he was second.

Barry bestrode the world of motorcycle racing again in 1977. This time he outraced and outsmarted Hennen again, and the American Stevie Baker on the Yamaha. Once more, Sheene was king.

This reign was abruptly ended the next year, however, when Kenny Roberts arrived, introducing new levels of competitiveness and, more importantly, new techniques of rear-wheel steering, both learned in the hard world of US dirt-track racing. Not that Barry didn't put up a good fight, beaten by only 10 points after complaining for most of the season of a debilitating virus infection. He claimed two wins to Roberts's four, although both of those were in races where his formidable new rival failed to finish.

The next year, his last on a factory Suzuki, brought three more race wins, but too many non-finishes, and he was third overall, behind Roberts and Virginio Ferrari. His popularity in Britain was still sky-high, boosted in no small measure by a truly heroic performance at his home GP. He was

Riding the bronco, Sheene was sixth at Imatra in Finland. Enough to secure his second crown.
(Henk Keulemans)

The class of '77: Sheene is on pole in Germany from Agostini's Yamaha and Suzuki team-mate Hennen. Although champion, he always stuck with the number 7.
(Henk Keulemans)

three-tenths of a second behind Roberts, but he'd been slowed by a back-marker on the final lap, and his valiant, vain last attack was wonderful to see. He won the *MCN* Man of the Year award for the fifth time (having finished second the year before to Mike Hailwood). Defiantly, he accepted the award wearing a Yamaha T-shirt. That was the end with Suzuki – but the factory Yamahas he'd hoped for were only for one man, Kenny Roberts, and although Barry did get some grudging factory help over the next three years, 14th and then fifth overall in 1980 and 1981 illustrate his problems clearly. It was not until the British GP of 1982 that Sheene was given a V4 500, like the one Roberts had been using, and after an overnight chassis rebuild, he was convinced he could win his home GP, and have a strong chance at the championship.

Instead, in mixed free practice at Silverstone the day before the meeting opened, Sheene had another catastrophic crash. Dicing with Jack Middleburgh, he ran at full speed into Patrick Igoa's fallen 250. Barry again suffered grievous injuries – to both legs at the knee, and to his left wrist. He was, in truth, lucky to survive, and equally lucky with the skill of the subsequent surgery.

Seven months later, Sheene was back on a racing 500, after a recovery that defied the odds, and showed yet again the strength of his fortitude and commitment. He was once more mounted on a Suzuki, but it was just a production model, albeit with a specially commissioned chassis, and the results again reflected its status – 14th overall in 1983, and sixth the next year, with a best of third at the Swedish GP. Sheene resisted one last temptation to join the Cagiva team, and retired at the end of 1984.

By 1983, Sheene was a hero for his courageous fight back from injury; Stephanie for nursing him to health. Little over a year later they would move to Australia to raise a family.
(Henk Keulemans)

In 1979, his last year on the factory Suzuki, Sheene added three race wins, missing out by a tenth of a second here in Holland. He was still a massive star everywhere he went.
(Henk Keulemans)

Sheene with his parents Iris and Frank and partner Stephanie in 1984, after announcing his retirement. (Phil Masters)

Former double Suzuki champion Barry Sheene, now a part-time TV guru, interviews 1993 Suzuki champion Kevin Schwantz and GP-winning team-mate Daryl Beattie. (Henk Keulemans)

Sheene on a Manx Norton? Barry returned to the track in 1999 as a, part-time, successful classic bike rider. (Phil Masters)

Sheene's trademark was a quick wit delivered with a cheery grin. (Phil Masters)

After retirement, and mindful of his many fractures, Sheene moved to the more comfortable climate of Australia, where he and his wife Stephanie raised two children. Barry also moved his collection of old racing bikes including the 125 Suzuki that had started it all, and (among many other things) he embarked on a new career as a typically frank and forthright TV commentator.

Sheene is an occasional GP visitor outside Australia, and at the end of the last century made a racing return, riding a Manx Norton in selected classic events, and taking just as much pleasure in his performance as ever.

Kenny Roberts Snr

Born
31 December 1951
Modesto, California, USA

500cc WORLD CHAMPIONSHIPS
1978 – Yamaha (Four wins: Austrian GP, French GP, Italian GP, British GP)

1979 – Yamaha (Five wins: Austrian GP, Italian GP, Spanish GP, Yugoslav GP, British GP)

1980 – Yamaha (Three wins: Italian GP, Spanish GP, French GP)

Total 500cc GP wins: 22

Point proved. Third at the last GP of the year at Germany's Nürburgring was enough to win Roberts the 500cc championship at his first attempt.
(Henk Keulemans)

When he arrived in GP racing in 1978, direct and outspoken to the point of rudeness, Kenny Roberts struck the blue-blazered establishment as something of a nuisance. This invader from the USA had a high opinion of his own ability – he didn't mind who knew it. And he had a low opinion of anyone who didn't respect racers and racing as much as he did. He seemed an unlikely candidate to become not just an elder statesman of racing, but a visionary and an unofficial monarch.

Now the blue blazers have been pushed to one side. Kenny not only conquered racing, he pushed on to become a top team owner, and a manufacturer in his own right. As well as all this, the maverick from far away had been instrumental in a series of changes that influenced the whole way racing was run.

This maverick king won three crowns in a row

And the high opinion of his ability? Well, it turned out to be less an opinion, more a typically deeply-considered analysis of the available data; and it was correct.

Kenny was not the first American racer to show the world that they knew something about how to ride a bike over there, even if they did tend to put their feet down in the corners, dirt-track style. The dirt tracks had also taught them to control a sliding bike, and to steer with the throttle. If that skill coincides with a time of vaulting power outputs and tyres that can't keep pace – well, that is when history gets written.

Cal Rayborn was the first American to make an impact on modern European racing, in 1972. Stevie Baker and Pat Hennen followed. Then came Kenny to take up the torch, to start a blaze that cast a new light on racing for decades to come.

Kenny had grown up in Modesto – one of the broad string of small

Kenny burst into world racing in 1978 after conquering America – and did the same thing to Europe. (Henk Keulemans)

Roberts and Sheene were the rivals from opposite sides of the Atlantic – here at Assen, and everywhere else as well. (Henk Keulemans)

towns running along California's Central Valley, a heartland of dirt-track racing. A small and sickly infant, he had a talent for survival. Life for the family was hard-working and tough, with few privileges. Except for his gift of an almost boundless talent for motorcycle racing. Luckily enough, Kenny also had the boundless confidence and enthusiasm that would have left him hurting if the talent hadn't been there. These three things don't always occur in such equal measure, even among the other great champions in this book.

He first raced in his early teens, his mother lying about his age so he could get entries at the local tracks where kids could chase their dreams round and round the endless oval. From the start, Kenny was special, prepared to try new lines and techniques, and he quickly built momentum, especially after a sympathetic nearby bike dealer and racing workshop owner started to help out. Kenny's first ever sponsor was a man called Bud Aksland, a member of a now famous racing family, and still today (as an engine development engineer) a key member of the Roberts dynasty.

With better machinery, Kenny started winning by such margins that local clubs instituted a special handicapping system, putting his 100cc bike up against the 250s. The way he was going, it was a short step from small-town tracks to the big-time, the AMA national circuit – a punishing zig-zag back and forth across the continent. He joined as a Novice in 1970, and by his second year was winning races in all the disciplines that counted to what was in those days a formidable Grand National Championship – mile and half-mile ovals, short-track, TT racing (dirt-track, with jumps), and road-racing, an increasingly important element.

As a Junior, Kenny had been recruited by Yamaha (or was it the other way round?), starting an association that was to last well beyond his retirement as a triple World Champion. The Japanese company was already a major road-racing force. With Kenny they took on a giant-killing challenge, tackling the mighty Harley-Davidson on its own territory. And Kenny – storming round the outside on the soft dirt 'cushion' or hanging it out round the pole (the apex) – rose to the occasion, wrestling the underpowered and under-developed Yamaha twin, based on a 650cc road bike, up against anyone, whatever their size.

Kenny's daring, indomitable, experimental dirt-track exploits made him a legend even before he became Grand National Champion in 1973, in his second year as a Senior, but the riders and bikes he (massively) outpointed show how success in road-racing was becoming increasingly important. Old

A historic moment, as Kenny Roberts crosses the Nürburgring finish line to become the first American World Champion. (Henk Keulemans)

dirt-track rival Gary Scott (Triumph) was second and dirt-track veteran Mert Lawill (Harley-Davidson) fourth, but third went to Gary Nixon, riding for Kawasaki, who didn't even build a dirt-tracker.

Kenny won it again the next year, with a record points score, and if he lost out to dirt-trackers over the next two years, this was only narrowly. Then it was time to move on – but not before one glorious, legendary swansong, at the Indianapolis mile, when Kenny's gang wheeled out a breath-taking answer to the rumbling Harleys ... a brakeless 750cc two-stroke flat-tracker, based on Yamaha's formidable TZ750 four-cylinder road-racer. Those who watched its lone outing reckoned nobody but Kenny could even ride it. Certainly nobody but Kenny could win on it, in what years later he would select as his greatest race – rooster-tailing out of the final turn with the motor screaming and the back tyre ripping the track to shreds, to surge past the two factory Harley-Davidsons of Korkie Keener and Jay Springsteen and take the flag. After one more race, at Kenny's insistence, the machine was banned.

He had already raced in Europe, starting in 1974 battling Ago at Imola, and at the British Trans-Atlantic series, where he had met golden boy Sheene for the first time – and beat him, with a fraction of the road-racing experience on unfamiliar tracks. In 1978, the Roberts wagon pulled into the GP pits, to stay.

Some measure of his confidence may be gauged from his mounting a 250 attack as well as the 500 (not to mention the F750 title too – one way to learn all the new tracks fast). Not even the old hands did that any more, let alone a rookie. He had with him former 250 champion Kel Carruthers, his road-race boss and mentor from Yamaha in the USA, and the backing of

Roberts only raced as hard as he had to at tracks like Imatra. Here he chases Japanese star Takazumi Katayama in 1980. (Henk Keulemans)

Silverstone – flowing and fast – was a favourite track. Here Roberts keeps company with Lucchinelli and race winner Randy Mamola in 1980. (Henk Keulemans)

the Yamaha factory – up to a point. The real factory rider was the 350 champion, Venezuelan Johnny Cecotto, and Kenny only had one 500 until the British GP at Silverstone, the penultimate of 11 rounds. That race was ruined by rain, as time-keepers lost count of who was leading and who was in the pits. A tainted victory was awarded to Kenny anyway – something which confirmed his low opinion of the way the sport was run. That opinion dropped still lower after races held on very dangerous tracks, like Imatra in Finland and the old Nürburgring, where he tied up a historic first title two weeks later, with a safe and rather grim-faced third. At his first attempt, the maverick had bearded Sheene and his cronies in their den.

Kenny's winning streak, if you want to call it that, went on for the next two years. All accomplished with his unique combination: a thoughtful approach, a daunting level of skill, and an utter dedication to winning. He was the first rider since Agostini to win three 500 titles in a row, and the feat was not repeated by anyone until his own protégé, Rainey, more than ten years later.

There had been some great moments along the way. The classic showdown between Kenny and Barry Sheene in 1979 was selected as one of BBC TV's 100 Great Sporting Moments. Kenny won, by inches. There'd been grimmer battles that year: a pre-season testing fall in Japan in 1978 had broken his back, and for a while he hadn't even been expected to defend his title.

Typically, Kenny was by now on to the next project. His concentration on racing, he would explain, was so total that it was compartmentalised. He had time to think about other things – including his increasing ire at the low status of riders within racing, and the conditions that they were obliged

Champions past, present and future – Roberts (Yamaha), Lucchinelli and Sheene (both Suzuki) fight it out in the 1981 French GP at sun-baked Paul Ricard circuit. Lucchinelli won the race, and the crown.
(Henk Keulemans)

to face, at disdainful rates of pay. His answer was typically maverick. Don't fight. Just strike off elsewhere, make something better. Thus the World Series was born. In the end, the plan to mount a rival independent televised championship, with big prize money and professional promotion, was strangled by the establishment. But not without far-reaching consequences that ultimately changed GP racing in exactly the same way that Kenny and his cohorts had originally planned in 1980.

So, Roberts came back to the GPs with the rest of the riders, and added another three wins as he out-pointed Mamola for a third title.

By now, Kenny's once-prickly reception in Europe had turned to respect. In the way of these things, it wasn't until he started to lose the championship that the adoration began. Kenny was beaten in 1981 and '82, more by a variety of circumstances than a pair of Italian semi-privateers. Then, in 1983, when his V4 Yamaha was made to feel (and sometimes look) clumsy and disjointed by the inspired Freddie Spencer on his agile three-cylinder Honda, Kenny's popularity was assured, as he tried everything he knew to fight off the challenge. Kenny now counts his greatest racing error from that year, in Sweden, when yet another desperate battle was decided under braking for the penultimate corner of the Anderstorp circuit. Freddie dived inside him and took both off on to the dirt. Freddie recovered first, won that race, and the title, by two points. Kenny's mistake: 'I under-estimated what he would be prepared to do.'

Kenny retired at the end of that season. He was troubled by Racer's Wrist (which causes the forearms to knot up painfully), and he'd given racing as much as he could as a rider. But he wasn't finished yet.

In 1984, he ran his first team – a low-budget 250 squad for protégé

In 1983, Agostini ran the team, Roberts rode the bikes, in his last racing season. (Henk Keulemans)

After retirement, Kenny first became a successful team owner, then a manufacturer. This is the Modenas he built, with riders Kenny Junior and Frenchman Jean-Michel Bayle, in 1997. (Henk Keulemans)

Rainey and Briton Allan Carter. Then he took a sabbatical, to regroup and 'come back and do this thing properly'. He returned in 1986 with big-bucks Lucky Strike backing for a second factory Yamaha squad (riders Randy Mamola and Mike Baldwin), and from there moved on to Marlboro money and the official factory Yamaha team, winning three 500 titles with Rainey, and one 250 crown with John Kocinski.

Kenny's team assembled an unprecedented number of top engineers, electronics experts, designers, tuners and mechanics. With this high-powered Team Roberts Think Tank, it is not surprising that he grew impatient with the Japanese system of leasing racing bikes, and keeping technical development in-house. At the end of each expensive season, you didn't even get to keep the bikes. Kenny had all the ingredients together for yet another bold move – taking on the might of Japan as an independent manufacturer.

The first four years of running the three-cylinder Modenas (something of a tribute to Spencer's vanquishing Honda of '83) were among the hardest in a life spent taking on the establishment. Teething troubles with the bike saw sponsorship backing, riders and even key team members melt away, while maverick Kenny once again found himself edged out of his former position of influence by new racing rights-holders Dorna. Being Kenny, he never did give up – and by the time the last year of the 500 class began, the renamed bike (Proton KR3) and the small tight-knit team seemed to have turned a corner, and threatened their most competitive season yet. Kenny's specially-built engineering base in Banbury was increasingly doing consulting engineering work for other teams, and was poised in the heart of England's famous 'F1 Belt' for the four-stroke era.

At the same time, he gave racing the next US champion, his elder son Kenny Junior, with yet another fast and maverick Roberts, younger son Kurtis, seeming set hot on his heels.

The legend of King Kenny is not over yet.

The fateful 1983 confrontation with Spencer awaits here in Sweden. Mechanics Nobby Clark and Fiorenzo Fanali hold his machines in readiness.
(Henk Keulemans)

Marco**Lucchinelli**

Born
26 June 1954
Ceparana, Italy

500cc WORLD CHAMPIONSHIP
1981 – Suzuki (Five wins:
French GP, Dutch TT,
Belgian GP, San Marino
GP, Finnish GP)

**Total 500cc GP
wins:** 6

*Marco Lucchinelli – nobody enjoyed
victory more. (Henk Keulemans)*

What a time it was in racing. The freedom explosion of the Sixties left a residual of post-hippie racers; with less than a dozen GPs a year and the F750 championship defunct, there were only a handful of international races, and time on your hands. The pay packets were getting bigger in the dawn of the modern era of fully sponsored racing, yet the old free spirit of motorbike racing was still a long way short of being cut and polished for the still forthcoming 'corporate image of the sport'.

Marco Lucchinelli's reputation was made in this era – and of all the fun-loving, party-crazy, girl-chasing racers of that time this long-haired Italian was the most prominent. Rather ostentatiously crazy off the track, Lucchinelli remained a calculating and highly effective racer once aboard a bike. By the time another noted long-haired crazy – Valentino's father

He out-rode and out-partied them all

Graziano Rossi – joined him as a team-mate in 1979, the self-styled 'Lucky' was maturing as a competitor. He had always been fast, but had suffered erratic results, as often as not with machine problems.

Lucchinelli had a meteoric rise after starting to race at the age of 20. Within a year he rode in his first GP at Imola; and soon after that he came to the attention of Roberto Gallina, a former racer now running high-level Suzukis. With little more than a year of road-racing experience, Lucchinelli was given the ride – and he made a big impression, finishing fourth overall. That year, 1976, Suzuki's definitive square four RG500 filled the first six places, and then went on all the way down to 12th, with Agostini seventh on a lone MV Agusta. Lucchinelli had proved from the start that he could be right up among the best of them.

Over the next few seasons, always on Suzukis but for a spell not with Gallina, Lucchinelli would generally be among the front runners, but too often out of the race by the end, so that it took him until 1979 before he claimed his first GP win. This was at a time, of course, when Kenny Roberts had arrived and raised the stakes. Lucchinelli went with him, but even so it was significant that his first win was at the title-deciding Nürburgring – the old Nürburgring, a track where Roberts, that year's third-time champion, steadfastly refused to race at full throttle.

The next year, however, he beat Roberts. Mounted on the trusty Gallina Suzuki, Lucchinelli swept to victory with five race wins. To be fair, Roberts was struggling on a new square-four Yamaha – fast but clumsy – while Barry Sheene had switched camps too and was riding for the most

Pals and rivals – Lucchinelli clowns with his helmet, while chatting to Kenny Roberts. (Henk Keulemans)

part a B-list Yamaha. Randy Mamola, on the official factory Suzuki, had no such excuse. Lucchinelli had outridden as well as outpartied them all. But it had not been easy.

The year began with a crash in Austria while disputing the lead at the Salzburgring. Marco was not hurt, but seemed to come back stronger, calmer and more mature. Over the course of the season the points lead went first to Mamola, and then to Roberts. Lucchinelli was to get more focused in the middle stage, taking a clear win from Mamola in the heat at Paul Ricard in France, a close second to the American in Yugoslavia, and then another win in the wet at Assen. Now Lucchinelli led on points for the first time, and the next race, the Belgian GP at Spa Francorchamps, was to prove pivotal.

On that daunting track in dire conditions – mixed wet and dry – Lucchinelli relentlessly closed on Roberts, who had a significant lead, then battled with him to the finish. At the final hairpin he got the better of a run round a lapped rider and won his third race in a row.

His fourth win came in front of rapturous home fans at Imola – but the title battle was far from over. At the next round at Silverstone, Lucchinelli was involved in a crash in the leading group after Graeme Crosby and Sheene collided. He remounted, but scored no points. And the points lead over Mamola shrank to just six, with two rounds remaining.

The first was at the distinctly scary public roads circuit at Imatra, north-east of Helsinki, right on the Russian border – it was lined with trees and telegraph poles, and was no place to fall off. 'I definitely ride at 80 per cent

Lucchinelli heels the Suzuki hard over in Finland in 1981. For one glorious year, he did everything right. (Henk Keulemans)

Leading former champions Roberts and Sheene at Paul Ricard, 'Lucky' is en route to victory in the French GP in his championship year. (Henk Keulemans)

Lucchinelli and the Italian mob: team boss Roberto Gallina is on the new champion's left. (Henk Keulemans)

Flying in Finland: Lucchinelli's year saw him peak on the Suzuki. A move to Honda the next season led nowhere. (Henk Keulemans)

here. I'm too young to die,' the American quipped at the time. Lucchinelli said nothing beyond showing flashes of temperament, and went out to take a decisive win.

When they got to Sweden for the final round he had a nine-point advantage, with 15 points for a win. Conditions were difficult again, with a drying track but more rain during the race. Mamola slowed as it got wetter, and the psychological turning point came as Lucchinelli, riding very cautiously, caught and overtook him. The championship, finally, was won.

The next year he was signed up to join Honda, bringing the number one plate to their fresh assault on the 500 class, following the failure of their

In 1982, Lucchinelli took the Number 1 plate to Honda but the sparkle was over. (Henk Keulemans)

NR500 four-stroke. He joined Freddie Spencer, Takazumi Katayama and Ron Haslam on the new three-cylinder two-stroke. In only the second race, while disputing the lead of the Austrian GP with Franco Uncini, Lucky crashed and, though not badly hurt, it seemed another turning point. A new Italian on a Gallina Suzuki was about to take over, and Lucchinelli never did win another GP, though he was twice more on the rostrum in his second year on the Honda.

Many said that the title had gone to his head – that his dedication to racing was lost, that he'd turned into a party animal instead. Lucchinelli did little to discourage this reputation. Volatile, expressive, noisy and full of fun (though exceedingly disputatious with any form of authority), he was certainly given to a very thorough enjoyment of the fruits of his success. Be that as it may, Lucchinelli's contract was not renewed at the end of 1983, and he dropped from view, until he found an opportunity to reinvent himself with Ducati, leading the way with a couple of wins in the Formula One series of 1986, and perfectly placed to bring the Italian factory into the new World Superbike championship of 1988. He won at the first round, and was in the title hunt until the end of the season. He retired at the end of that year to take over management of the Ducati team, and two years later was in charge when Raymond Roche won the first of the marque's string of riders' titles in the four-stroke class.

The gainsayers seemed justified when in 1991 Lucchinelli was convicted on cocaine charges, but he returned to racing again as a team manager in 1999, with Ducati's R&D team. In between times, he is the co-owner and habituee of a lively late-night bar in Imola, where he will always be World Champion.

The good, the bad, and the Lucky.
(Phil Masters)

Victory is sweet – and Lucchinelli, here with Joey Dunlop, enjoyed every aspect of it. (Phil Masters)

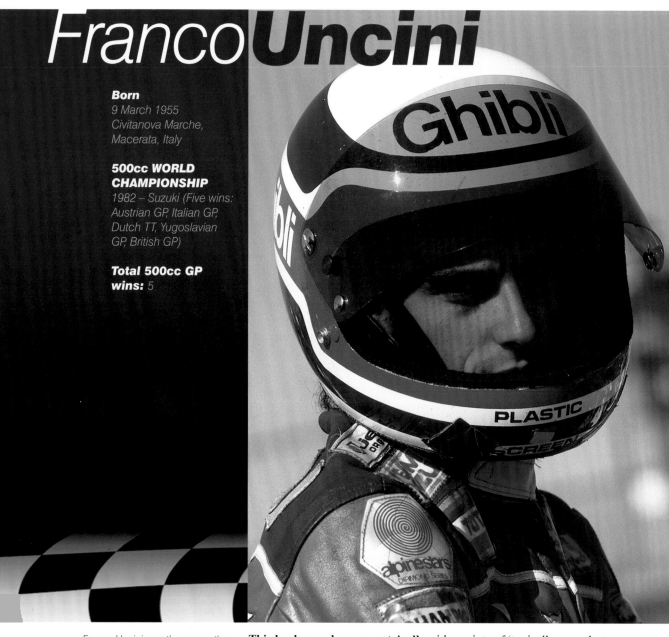

Franco Uncini

Born
9 March 1955
Civitanova Marche,
Macerata, Italy

500cc WORLD CHAMPIONSHIP
1982 – Suzuki (Five wins:
Austrian GP, Italian GP,
Dutch TT, Yugoslavian
GP, British GP)

Total 500cc GP wins: 5

Franco Uncini won the crown, then came back from the dead.
(Henk Keulemans)

This book reveals an eccentrically wide variety of 'typical' racers, but Franco Uncini was not one of them. Quiet and gentlemanly by breeding as well as nature, the darkly handsome youth turned his back on a career in the family ceramics business to go racing, and had to conquer considerable opposition. It was his obvious skill that tipped the balance and prevented a family rift. He first raced at the age of 19. Two years later he was in the GPs as a 250–350 privateer, and immediately making a mark. Franco was fast, and if he crashed rather too often for comfort then one needed only to recall the racing dictum: that it's easier for a fast rider who crashes to learn how to stop crashing than it is for a safe rider to learn to go faster.

The Italian (ex-Cagiva) Harley-Davidson team obviously thought so too. They hired Franco to ride alongside defending champion Walter Villa in the 250 and 350 classes. The youngster outranked his senior team-mate, finishing second in the 250 class. He spent one more year in the smaller classes, a privateer again, with Villa alone on the Harley for its final season.

It was time to move on, and in 1979 the 500 class was relatively welcoming compared with today. The factory bikes ruled, but the private square-four RG500 Suzuki was capable of running them close, and now and then even beating them. Uncini joined the gang of Suzuki 500 riders, and proved from the start that he was one of the good guys, claiming a best finish of third in Yugoslavia, a technical track that favoured his classic, smooth style. He was also improving his finishing record. At 24, his challenge was maturing – but he still had to wait, until the year after Lucchinelli had won a solid championship on the Gallina Suzuki and then jumped ship.

Franco Uncini shakes the spray with Barry Sheene – first and third in Yugoslavia in 1982. (Henk Keulemans)

A serious approach – Uncini in the pits at Assen. (Henk Keulemans)

Abandoned, Roberto Gallina was mortified. Franco was his weapon of revenge. And, in a year when Kenny Roberts was again battling a difficult bike, and newcomer Freddie Spencer still feeling his way on the new three-cylinder Honda, Franco rode with superlative consistency. He took over the points lead from Roberts at home in Italy, the fifth of 12 rounds, and the Italian's second victory of the year. He went on to rack up a total of five, and continued to forge ahead. By the time they got to Britain for the ninth round, Franco was 20 points clear of Roberts and Barry Sheene.

Silverstone was Uncini's last win of the year. Sheene was eliminated for the rest of the year in a horrific pre-race crash, and Roberts fell on the first lap, ruining the rest of his season. Franco didn't finish another race – retiring with mechanical trouble in Sweden, hurting from a practice crash at

Intelligent racer with the gift of tact

Mugello, and crashing out of the German GP. No matter. The job was done.

Uncini, in his first year on a factory 500, had come somewhat out of the blue. It was the likes of Sheene and Roberts – and now Spencer – who were the racing establishment, and the fact that Lucchinelli had done much the same the year before only made it more of a surprise. As a result, there were those who said he'd been lucky; that he only won because of the misfortunes of others. A view that rather overlooked the fact that Uncini had not only achieved his race wins before injury eliminated his rivals, but that he'd been totally consistent, finishing all of the first nine races apart from the boycotted French GP, and in the top three every time except in the first round in Argentina, where he'd been fourth. And this was in a year with more works bikes and riders than ever.

Franco had his own reply to the critics, and wrote at the time: 'I did not consider that I was lucky this year. But I was not unlucky.'

Franco made his mark also for his obvious intelligence and stature. He seemed blessedly free from the fits of temperament that sometimes marked out his countrymen. Long before he was a championship contender he was already working as riders' representative, chosen as the man most able to articulate the many grievances of the time.

His reign as champion was brief, however. Halfway into the next year, still on the Gallina Suzuki, he was having a lean time as Roberts and Spencer drew ahead in their great battle. At Assen, on the second lap, he was lying fifth, as good as it had been all season. Then he tried too hard, the bike spun and slid sideways, and flicked him over the high-side into the path of the oncoming racers. He was not hurt, and quickly got to his hands and knees to run to the side of the track. At exactly the same time Wayne Gardner, in his first GP, swerved out to the same side. Uncini was struck by the front of the Honda, his helmet split open and came off, and he spun to a stop, deeply unconscious. Early reports were that he had been killed, and they were entirely plausible given the severity of the collision. Then news

Uncini took over the Gallina Suzuki from title winner Lucchinelli (here on the Number 1 Honda in Austria), and continued the team's winning streak. (Henk Keulemans)

Straining at the leash in Spain – Uncini will finish third at Jarama, behind Roberts and Sheene. (Henk Keulemans)

Classic Spa action – Uncini, Roberts, Sheene and Crosby at the 1982 Belgian GP. The race went to a newcomer, Fast Freddie Spencer. (Henk Keulemans)

Uncini and team-mate Loris Reggiani survey their winning blue bikes. (Henk Keulemans)

came that he was alive, but in a deep coma, in a critical condition.

Miraculously, if slowly, he made a complete recovery. 'I think it is because I was so fit,' he told me later. And he even came back to race again, for two more years in 1984 and 1985. By then the Suzuki was past its best years, even though Gallina made strenuous efforts, including a new chassis, to prolong its competitive life. The best Franco could manage was a single fifth place, and he retired at the end of the 1985.

It is right that such a well-rounded and well-respected individual should not be lost to racing, and before too much longer Franco was back at the GPs. Once again his role was that of riders' safety representative, a difficult balancing act that he has accomplished with tact and skill ever since.

Happy families? Roberto Gallina's title-winning pair, Marco Lucchinelli and his successor Franco Uncini. (Henk Keulemans)

Freddie Spencer

Born
20 January 1962
Shreveport, Louisiana,
USA

500cc WORLD CHAMPIONSHIPS
1983 – Honda (Six wins:
South African GP, French
GP, Italian GP, Spanish
GP, Yugoslavian GP,
Swedish GP)

1985 – Honda (Seven
wins: Spanish GP, Italian
GP, Austrian GP, Belgian
GP, French GP, British GP,
Swedish GP)

**Total 500cc GP
wins:** 20

Other titles
1985 – 250cc World
Champion

*Fresh-faced and fresh from the
Louisiana Bible Belt, Freddie Spencer
became the youngest ever 500 World
Champion at 21. (Henk Keulemans)*

Every champion in this book is extraordinary, but even here, Frederick Burdette Spencer stands out. Fast Freddie (was ever a nickname more appropriate?) rewrote the record book: on the way up, and on the way down again.

Aged 21 – fresh-faced and full of Bible Belt innocence, he was the youngest-ever 500 Champion. He was also Honda's first-ever champion in the class – succeeding where the likes of Hailwood and Redman had failed. He was the only rider in the modern era to win titles in two classes in the same year – 250 and 500 in 1985. His rise through world racing was meteoric, and for a time it seemed as though his domination would be complete.

What goes up must come down, however. Fat Freddie, as the unkinder

Dazzling star who soon fell to earth

Not always glorious – mud-spattered Freddie Spencer checks his extremities for damage after he was knocked off in the rain at Assen in 1985. The sequence shows Frenchman Christian Sarron triggering the first-lap crash.
(Henk Keulemans)

commentators called him, made one come-back and then another … both ending more or less disastrously, and certainly embarrassingly. The rider who had burned so bright in his early twenties fizzled out almost as quickly, and it was as much of a relief when he finally retired as it had been an exultation to watch him when he had been at the peak of his extraordinary powers.

And that is the way we should remember Fast Freddie. How could it be otherwise? For those of us there to watch, one thing must forever remain unforgettable – the sight of Freddie Spencer on his Rothmans Honda, leaping away from the front row of the grid and immediately seizing an early lead so commanding that it was very seldom that even the redoubtable Eddie Lawson could do much more than hold the gap in second place.

Freddie didn't so much ride the Honda as dance with it – or at least make it dance, all 185 unruly horsepower of it. The revvy, warbling V4 would skitter and slide, clearly on the brink of a big crash but for Spencer, sitting apparently serenely on top. Freddie could fight hard too, as he showed against Roberts in 1983, but in later years he developed some disdain for elbow-to-elbow work. His racing became all about the deployment of the most consummate technique, learned through what was literally a full lifetime of racing, much of which had taken place before he was ten years old. His fast starts and unrivalled ability to go very fast on cold tyres were a result of those dirt-track years – learning to adapt quickly to conditions, when the grip of the oval-track surface might change from one lap to the next, let alone from the heat in the morning to the final in the afternoon. 'The races were so short that if you didn't find the best way right away, you'd lost,' he told me. Another example was an advanced riding technique that he seems to have pioneered or at least taken to its final conclusion – the heavy use of the rear brake with the throttle open to control wheelspin.

Freddie was another product of America's 'On Any Sunday' generation, who'd discovered his gift on the thriving schoolboy dirt tracks of the Sixties and early Seventies. It was a family thing: father Freddie Senior was still racing and his 16-year-old brother was forging ahead in karts when the six-year-old Freddie first took to the tracks on a Briggs & Stratton minibike bought out of the Sears catalogue. 'We didn't take family vacations,' he told me later. 'We just went racing.'

Unlike the swathes of precocious talent that boiled up out of the California Crucible – all learning off one another – he was from the other

Cordial – for the moment. Title rivals Spencer and Roberts, before their pivotal Swedish showdown in 1983. (Henk Keulemans)

Fast Freddie Spencer stands on the podium top step for the first of 20 times in a four-year span, after winning the 1982 Belgian GP from Sheene and eventual champion Franco Uncini. (Henk Keulemans)

side of the continent, and something of a lone figure in the extent of his gift. But there were plenty of chances to polish this. At 10, he held State titles in Texas, Oklahoma, Arkansas, Mississippi and Louisiana. Before he turned 13 he was already racking up 100 sundry dirt-track races a year. And winning almost nine out of every ten.

Freddie turned pro at 16, just as soon as he could, armed with ten years of hard experience not only of motorcycle control on all sorts of surfaces, but also of how to win races and championships, rather than just turning fast laps. How to focus.

He won the Novice title in 1978 and the next year the AMA Lightweight title. By now, instead of just the family team, Freddie had joined up with the noted Japanese-American tuner and racing guru Erv Kanemoto. A world-beating partnership was born as Freddie carried on piling up the experience, now on tarmac – competing not only on TZ250 and TZ750 two-strokes, but also on a Ducati 900SS and on a Kawasaki Superbike, running up to ten races a day, including the heats and final.

Later that same year came Stage Two in this rocket-boost career. Honda USA lost their top Superbike rider Mike Baldwin to injury; Freddie was drafted in to the team – and straight away won two AMA nationals. For 1980, just 18, Freddie was signed up directly to the factory, who knew a good thing when they saw one.

The new year also took Freddie out of the USA for the first time – at Easter to the Trans-Atlantic races, where he and the silver Kanemoto Yamaha TZ750 were the new sensation of a strong and easily victorious US team including Roberts and Randy Mamola. He and Kanemoto also ran their first GP, in Belgium – Spencer retiring his uncompetitive production

The final battle: Roberts and Spencer duel at Imola in the 1983 San Marino GP. To Roberts the race, to Spencer the kingdom.
(Henk Keulemans)

Japanese-American tuner Erv Kanemoto was crucial to Spencer's success. Here rival Roberts completes the triangle in 1983.
(Henk Keulemans)

Yamaha after qualifying 12th. The main focus was on US racing, where his too-fragile Honda finished third overall. Freddie stayed on in the USA in 1981, aiming at a Grand National title on Honda's road-racers and their rather nasty flat-tracker, wrought from the despatch riders' favourite road bike, the shaft-driven CX500. Outgunned in all departments, he finished third. Freddie rode Honda's ill-starred 32-valve four-stroke NR500 to its one and only win in the USA, then came to his second GP, in Britain, and on the four-stroke challenger for its last public outing. Exploiting the full 22,000rpm of the oval-piston V4, Spencer had it up as high as fifth when the motor cried 'enough'.

Now it was time for the World Championship. Spencer's début season of 1982 coincided with Honda's final capitulation to the two-stroke engine. HRC succumbed to the inevitable by scrapping the complex NR and showing up with its opposite – the simple, light three-cylinder NS500 V3. In the bike's and rider's break-in year, Freddie claimed four pole positions, four lap records, two race wins, and third place overall. He had arrived.

In 1983, Spencer and Roberts treated the world to a display of motorcycle racing, and rivalry, of the highest order. Head to head with the King in his final year, Freddie proved tough in a way that contradicted his choirboy looks and mild manners. The season was played out over 12 rounds, and the battle wasn't over until the last of them.

Each rider had claimed six wins, and each had fallen victim to bad luck and mechanical problems. More revealing was the way the previously

Solitude at La Source – Spencer spent much of 1985 alone like this, usually miles in the lead, on both 500 and 250 Hondas. (Henk Keulemans)

In 1984, teething troubles with Honda's new V4 meant a hard year for Freddie, but in 1985 the combination was strong again. Here he has just won in Spain, the second round, from Lawson and Sarron. He was again at the height of his powers. (Henk Keulemans)

complete Kenny seemed to come loose at the seams – like a silly crash at Monza, caught out by back-markers, remounting only to run out of fuel; and the incident in Sweden described in Kenny's profile in this book. There was a team blunder in Yugoslavia where, had Lawson been told to slow down, Kenny would have picked up another place. The outcome of the year might have been different in each case, for the final margin in Spencer's favour was only two points.

Freddie's next year was blighted by minor injuries, and the many quirks of Honda's all-new four-cylinder NSR – including the collapse of a carbon-fibre wheel while practising for the first race. But 1985 was a triumph. With Roberts retired, and defending champion Lawson still in 'Steady Eddie' mode, Freddie swung into action with a double-header challenge, supplementing his 500 with Honda's all-new NSR250. He won both titles with races to spare, adding another seven wins in each class to his tally to become the first rider to win the 500cc and another championship in the same year since Agostini won the 500 and 350 in 1972.

Freddie was supreme. First away, fast for ever, marvellous to see. What went wrong after that? Everything. Freddie ran out of physical strength with a series of injuries and a bad case of Racer's Wrist. He seemed also to run out of motivation, having achieved so much by the age of only 23, telling me: 'I don't see myself racing motorcycles into my late twenties'. Two more years with Honda saw a steady decline, and at the beginning of 1988 Spencer announced his retirement.

A landmark talent, Freddie Spencer found new ways to get the best out of the frighteningly powerful Honda V4 – the first of the final generation of 500cc racers. (Henk Keulemans)

Spencer's 500/250 double in 1985 was a brilliant final flash in a meteoric career. He never did find the combination again. (Henk Keulemans)

If only he had left it at that. But when Agostini, desperate for a big name to replace the departed Lawson on the 1989 factory Yamaha, called him up, Freddie took the bait. He did claim one fifth place, but Freddie had gained weight and lost (it seemed) all his greatness. The team did not last the year, the two ex-champions 'mutually agreeing' to part before the end of the European season. And that was not all. Freddie returned to race Superbikes in the USA, never regaining his earlier form, then – leaner and fitter – returned to the 500 class in 1993, riding for Yamaha France. He seemed at least to be serious about 'changing the way I left racing'. But heavy crashes in the first two races left him injured, and although he returned at the end of the year to score two last points in Italy, another crash a fortnight later at the US GP ended it all.

It would be harsh to dwell on the protracted end to the relatively short career of a rider who, when at his best, had been compared to Hailwood. But Fast Freddie's memory needs no charity. His star had shone so brightly that for it to fade was only a way of restoring the natural balance.

After his retirement, Freddie founded a road-racing school in Las Vegas, which he runs to this day.

Erv Kanemoto and Freddie Spencer – their partnership was devastating.
(Henk Keulemans)

By 1987, Spencer (19) was a shadow of his former self. The effort had taken more out of the youngster than anybody had realised. He could still start fast, however – leading lap one in Britain from Ron Haslam (9), Lawson (1), Gardner (2) and the rest.
(Henk Keulemans)

Eddie Lawson

Born
11 March 1958
Upland, California

500cc WORLD CHAMPIONSHIPS
1984 – Yamaha (Four wins: South African GP, Spanish GP, Austrian GP, Swedish TT)

1986 – Yamaha (Seven wins: Italian GP, West German GP, Austrian GP, Yugoslav GP, French GP, Swedish TT, San Marino GP)

1988 – Yamaha (Seven wins: US GP, Portuguese GP, Italian GP, Austrian GP, French GP, Swedish TT, Brazilian GP)

1989 – Honda (Four wins: Spanish GP, Belgian GP, French GP, Swedish TT)

Total 500cc GP wins: 31

Steady Eddie? Four times champion Lawson kept his own counsel, and carved a niche in history. (Phil Masters)

It is in the nature of motorcycle champions to be independent-minded. But in this respect, few of the other 500 champions in this book can hold a candle to Eddie Lawson. Aloof from mundane considerations, scornful of the peripheral demands of being a racer (from sponsors, press or fans), dedicated to achieving the maximum without exceeding himself or his machine, the quiet, intelligent Californian was sometimes under-rated as a result. His last word on the subject was his fourth title in 1989, achieved after a breathtakingly unexpected change of horses shortly before the start of the year. A Yamaha man throughout his 500-class GP career, in that year Lawson took long-time colleagues and rivals totally by surprise, switching to a specially formed independent factory Honda team.

The 1989 bike was not good, as demonstrated by the struggles of

Steady progress from crucible to crowns

regular rider Wayne Gardner and newcomer Mick Doohan. The almost superhuman efforts of Lawson and team leader Erv Kanemoto, working doggedly through a year during which they received more than 15 new frames in a relentless quest, Lawson eventually pegged back his career-long shadow Wayne Rainey in a bitter-end finale in Sweden. Lawson was the first rider to win titles on different machines since Agostini and Duke, the only one to do so back-to-back. To anybody who really understands racing, the stature of this remarkable rider could have had no more trenchant proof.

Lawson was a couple of years ahead of Rainey in the thriving pre-teen motorcycle culture that prevailed in southern California in the early Seventies. He and Wayne were not the only World Champions to come out of that LA Crucible. Asked just what it was that made the standard so high, Lawson's reply is typically dry, as he reels off a string of names of dusty minor and major-league names of tracks in and around Los Angeles: 'Trojan, Ascot, Saddleback, Elsinore, Corona, Indian Dunes, Paris Raceway, Carlsbad ... We could race seven nights a week if we wanted, and for years we almost did. And we got good.'

It wasn't just a chance for a youngster to learn all the basics of racing on loose surfaces to a very high standard. It was also a place to get noticed. Thus it was that Shell Thuett, a dirt-track mentor to Kenny Roberts Senior among many others, picked on Eddie when he was looking for a junior rider; thus it was also that Kawasaki – in a similar position – gave Eddie the next step forward. In each case, as he matured enough to merit a junior team-mate of his own, who should it be but his old Corona and Indian Dunes riding mate – the guy he'd sometimes practised with, hour after hour on deserted oil rigs when he was perfecting the art of the prolonged power slide – Wayne Rainey.

Lawson was paving a path to the top. It was a slightly different route from that taken by Roberts before him, since US racing had changed in the

Eddie rides the Yamaha's power band in Belgium in 1984. He won four races to Spencer's five. More importantly, he scored good points in every single race of the year.
(Henk Keulemans)

meantime with the sudden rise of Superbikes. The combined discipline of dirt-track and road-racing had been separated in 1976, and Lawson was one of the few that made the cross-over easily, having already tasted road-racing with some good showings on Kawasaki's 250 GP bike on US tracks.

Quiet and self-effacing, Eddie slipped into the maturing Superbike series in 1980, winning first time out at Talladega, and in 1981 narrowly beat Freddie Spencer and Wes Cooley for the first of two consecutive national titles. Kawasaki did well out of Eddie Lawson replicas of his winning green machine, but the rider had moved on – taken into Yamaha's 500 GP squad in support of defending champion Kenny Roberts. It was the deep end. Roberts, in his final year, was engaged tooth and nail with Spencer. Lawson, still finding his feet on a 500 two-stroke on strange circuits, was expected to ride shot-gun to this pair.

The next year, Lawson was ready to show what a double US Superbike champion was made of. Justifying his nickname of Steady Eddie, he made a counterpoint to the mercurial defending champion Freddie Spencer and his fast but flawed new four-cylinder Honda. Spencer won five races to Lawson's four, but the title was Lawson's by a good margin – thanks to the fact that he finished every other race in the top four, including four second places. Eddie had shown that Steady could be relentlessly effective, if it was done fast enough.

Eddie and Freddie were the main event over the next two years. In 1985 Freddie won out by just eight points. The win ratio this time was seven: three in Spencer's favour, but again Lawson's relentless string of top-four finishes pushed the battle to the finish, keeping Spencer honest in the year he was also stretched by winning the 250 title. There was one non-finish this year – an uncharacteristic fall on a wet white line at Assen. Since Spencer was already out of the same race, knocked down by Frenchman Christian Sarron, it didn't affect the title position.

Lawson's dry sense of humour meant some thought him a laid-back and casual character. In fact, his dedication was second to none. (Henk Keulemans)

By 1986, Lawson was still devastatingly consistent, and riding the now familiar Yamaha better than ever. (Phil Masters)

All the while Lawson stuck to his game plan – reeling off one accurate lap after another, while keeping his own counsel. Spencer was definitely the more glamorous, but that hardly bothered Lawson, at least outwardly. It was a year later when he finally did make an acid comment to me – though that was not about Spencer, but about the press's lionisation of him after an incident in Rijeka. Spencer had clipped a corner apex-bale with his knee, raced to second in agony, and was hailed as a hero after being lifted off the bike at the finish. Eddie's view: 'It was also possible to miss the bale.' In the same interview, asked what was Spencer's weak point, he replied, as dryly: 'He doesn't take me seriously. My strong point is that I do.'

The rematch in 1986 didn't take place, with Spencer's career coming to an abrupt end. Lawson's new Honda rival was Wayne Gardner, and he defeated the relatively inexperienced Australian comfortably enough. Typically, he made it look easy. As typically, when Gardner prevailed the next year, Lawson kept on pushing in his own way. Then it was an even-numbered year – Eddie's turn again, by the law of things. In a season enlivened by the arrival of Schwantz and Rainey, Gardner was again his closest rival, and a fierce one, but Lawson equalled his seven wins of the 1986 season, and was invincible. He was, I recall writing at the time, at the height of his powers.

I was wrong: 1989 was Eddie's year. Unhappy at what he perceived as Yamaha's tendency towards complacency each time they won, tired of only winning every other year, and with that independent streak nagging away, he began secret negotiations with Honda and Spencer's ex-crew chief Erv Kanemoto to put together their own independent team, with full factory backing. The news broke only a couple of days after he'd been to the Yamaha factory to look at his proposed new bike for 1989: he certainly

Three-times champion Lawson switched from Yamaha to Honda in 1989 and found a new challenger in former training mate Wayne Rainey. In Sweden, Rainey pushed and pushed. Until he crashed – giving the overall advantage to Eddie.
(Henk Keulemans)

1989 was a year of classic rivalry between three Americans on three different makes of motorcycle. Lawson (Honda), Rainey (Yamaha) and Schwantz (Suzuki) rode the wheels off them, often close enough to touch. This battle, at the German GP, saw Rainey beat Lawson by three tenths of a second after almost 40 minutes of racing.
(Henk Keulemans)

took them by surprise. Likewise Wayne Gardner, who until then had thought himself HRC's top man. He vowed revenge, but injury spiked his guns. In fact, Lawson's challenge this year would come from Yamaha, and from the man who had dogged his footsteps all the way from the Ontario speedway.

If Lawson was shocked by his new motorcycle, he said little and simmered quietly in the corner of the pit. Compared with the well-balanced Yamaha, the Honda may have been fast, but this year's version was a typical HRC special, with horsepower and top speed the god, and chassis an afterthought.

Kanemoto's status gave him a hot line to HRC and the capacity to experiment. All year long 'we threw chassis at the bike' he said later. There were more than a dozen variations, including a bizarre double-decker – the existing main chassis members reinforced with another layer of extrusion welded on the top. And as Eddie fought to get the bike harnessed to the track, Rainey made hay. He led on points all the way to the end of the European season. By then, however, Erv's relentless development and Eddie's steady riding was starting to pay dividends, both on the machine and in the results. Rainey was hardly less consistent. The old duelling mates went to Anderstorp for the Swedish GP with Rainey six points in front, with two last races to follow.

By now, Lawson had tamed the bike so he could use his technique of very early throttle opening mid-corner. At the Swedish TT this was Rainey's undoing. Lawson, nursing his tyres, had closed down the Yamaha's early lead by half distance. The pair pulled away from Sarron and Schwantz, then Lawson took the lead. The two held formation, Rainey sizing up his rival for a final attack. Then with one lap left, Rainey copied Lawson's throttle feed on the corner onto the long airstrip straight. It was more than his tyres could take, and he was high-sided abruptly off the top of the world. Lawson took the lead on points. And went on to become, once again, 500cc World Champion.

There was more to come, but it was in the nature of a diversion as his career wound towards its natural end. Lawson found the perfect running-mates for his independent streak in Cagiva, the lame ducks of the 500 class. In two years, with Lawson forcing a new combination of focus, determination and logic, the all-red Italian V4 was transformed into a seriously competitive motorcycle. Fittingly, it was in Lawson's hands that the marque gained the first of its three victories – in Hungary, after a lucky tyre gamble and a typically obdurate ride. Lawson must share the credit for the bike's other wins, over the next two years, ridden by John Kocinski, for it was Lawson who turned the sick man of racing into a respectable force.

When Lawson retired at the end of 1992, he left racing without a backward glance. 'He was a bit bashful,' is how Shell Thuet saw it, all those years ago, at the start of a legend. He remained intensely private through a short but impressive IndyCar career, and later dedicated himself to a lighter form of motorsport, kart racing, where he racks up race wins and titles with just the same quiet and fearsome determination as he brought to motorcycles. Among his competitors is Wayne Rainey, for whom Lawson commissioned a hand-controlled kart almost directly after his Los Angeles crucible companion suffered paralysing injuries. For the first time ever, Rainey is obliged to accept second. For Eddie, first is still everything.

Lawson's Honda of 1989 was a wayward beast, with more horsepower than horse sense. Working with Spencer's ex-guru Kanemoto, the animal was turned into a winner.
(Henk Keulemans)

Wayne **Gardner**

Born
11 October 1959
Wollongong, New South
Wales, Australia

**500cc WORLD
CHAMPIONSHIP**
1987 – Honda (Seven
wins: Spanish GP, Italian
GP, Austrian GP, Yugoslav
GP, Swedish TT,
Czechoslovakian GP,
Brazilian GP)

**Total 500cc GP
wins:** 18

*True grit – nobody brought more
courage and determination to the party
than Australia's first 500 champion
Wayne Gardner.* (Henk Keulemans)

His nickname – one of them – was 'Digger', and it worked on several levels. He was Australian. His name was Gardner. But the most apposite of all was that nobody would dig deeper into his own resources, plundering emotion and courage to leave himself tearful and spent after many a great performance. Wayne's definitive Grand Prix may not have been one of the 18 where he claimed victory against all odds. Not even the Australian GP of 1990, where he almost crashed, breaking the fairing loose, then came back to pip Doohan for a second home-race victory.

His bike was damaged also at Suzuka in 1992, after a muddy slip-off in the rain-soaked race. Pressing on regardless, the remounted Digger was gaining ground hand over fist, riding in a zone where determination somehow meant more than tyre grip and engine performance. Never say

Digging for victory against wild odds

die, and never give up if there's even a glimmer of a chance. Not, in this case, of victory – team-mate Doohan was long gone. But the new Big Bang Honda made hay of the backmarkers, and Wayne had his sights on taking fifth from Mamola's Yamaha. And fifth is always better than sixth.

The crash was a cruncher, into the barrier after the bike had knocked the protective foam rubber out of the way. Gardner broke his leg yet again, and was out for the first half of his last season. He did claim one more emotional win, in Britain, after already having announced he would quit at the end of the year. Battered but still in one piece, the Wollongong Wild One had reached the end of a rough road to glory.

Wollongong Wild One was another nickname, earned as the brave and

In his second year as a full-time GP racer, Gardner was in at the deep end on the fearsome Honda NSR V4. He won three races. This is the Dutch TT of 1986.
(Henk Keulemans)

Wayne's girlfriend – and later wife – Donna was a constant support as he climbed the world racing ladder. Here, in 1986, he has almost reached the top. (Henk Keulemans)

reckless terror of the teenage Australian dirt-track scene. He never did manage to shake it off, throughout a career that led to a single 500 class championship at a time when the levels of riders and riding set new standards. Off the track, he did his dutiful best to serve the new 'corporate image of the sport', but his riding told the same old story. Often the fastest person on the track, he was never the neatest. Gardner would get into the most dreadful-looking scrapes, and then keep fighting the bike until he'd found a way out of them again. Until his luck turned towards the end of his dramatic career.

Born to a working class family in the steel town of Wollongong in New South Wales, Gardner was a speed-mad larrikin kid who later admitted that his gang stole and sold spare parts to buy petrol for his home-made

Australian engineer Jerry Burgess headed Gardner's title-winning crew. Here he talks to his first 500 champion. Later he was crew chief for Mick Doohan, and then Valentino Rossi. (Henk Keulemans)

go-kart. His first motorcycle was an old wreck he rebuilt himself, and he never looked back, earning his wings in junior dirt-tracking after trying and rejecting trials as too slow. The Wild One was soon the boy to beat in the lively teenage short-track scene.

He was 14 when he started racing, just 17 when a friend persuaded him to try road-racing. A few laps on a GP 250 two-stroke and he was hooked. At first, his win-or-crash style caused dismay, but he escaped an official ban, managed to calm down, and over the next couple of years made a name in Australian racing, muscling big production-based four-strokes round tight tracks. One such win – beating full race bikes in the wet – caught the eye of Japanese Kawasaki tuner and entrant Mamoru Moriwaki, who promptly hired Gardner for a season on four-strokes in Britain. On the sit-up-and-beg 'Streetbike', Wayne was spectacular. That was in 1981, and for 1982 Wayne was signed up for the Honda Britain team, to contest the highly active home four-stroke racing scene. He lived in Lincolnshire – when he wasn't sleeping in his car.

By 1983 the Australian was the dominant figure in British racing, and not only on four-strokes like the TT F1 Honda that won him the national title in 1983 and 1984. At the time, there was also a domestic 500

Austria's dauntingly fast Salzburgring circuit brought eventual victory to Gardner over Yamaha-mounted rival Randy Mamola – the third of seven wins that year for the title-winning Australian, now riding the full factory V4 Honda. (Henk Keulemans)

Jerez, 1987, and the Spanish GP gave Wayne his first win of the year, ahead of defending champion Lawson's Yamaha. (Henk Keulemans)

championship. Honda had a three-cylinder 500 that he used not only to take the title in 1984, but more importantly to master the art of sliding a two-stroke GP racer.

Gardner stayed with the team for 1985 as well, and his constant nagging to go GP racing (he had even funded a few 1984 outings from his own pocket) bore fruit. Rothmans-backed, Honda Britain contested the full season.

Wayne's long-standing ambition to be World Champion had survived a shocking and inauspicious start in his first GP at Assen in 1983, when he collided with and almost killed the fallen Franco Uncini. Two years later, the full-time rider was fourth overall, robbed of a first-year race win by a chunking tyre at Le Mans. He also won the Eight-Hour race for a second of three times, adding to his kudos with Honda. In 1986 he was taken into the full factory team on a four-cylinder NSR, to ride alongside Spencer ... until Spencer pulled out with wrist and motivation problems, leaving Gardner to bear the full burden of Honda's racing dreams.

Wayne went on to win three times, finishing second to Lawson and talking typically tough about how he would easily beat the American on an equal bike. As typically, he made good those threats in 1987, a year when Honda had resisted for once the temptation to put horsepower above road-

Gardner leads Lawson and Sarron at the 1988 French GP at Paul Ricard, one of the closest ever races. The defending champion had pulled clear at the finish ... only for his bike to blow an oil seal. He limped in an angry fourth, behind Lawson, Sarron and Schwantz. (Henk Keulemans)

holding. Gardner swept to seven wins out of 15 races, also taking ten lap records and ten pole-position starts. All done in trademark bullish style, in no way intimidated either by the opposition or the fearsome Honda. He sealed Australia's first ever World Championship in the premier class over the Yamahas of Mamola and Lawson.

From then on, things went downhill. Honda's 1988 bike was a handful on which he struggled and crashed, but still ran Lawson close. In 1989, he was already disgruntled when Rothmans hired Mick Doohan as his new team-mate – one top Australian being enough, in his view. Then, to his shock and dismay, Honda hired rival Lawson as a separate but equal factory rider. The confrontation might have become a racing classic. Instead, Gardner broke his leg badly in America, just a week after a home win in the inaugural Australian GP, and his challenge was ruined by yet more injury. He did not win another race that year.

Both these two rivals were facing new opposition by now – from Schwantz and Rainey, and of course Doohan. These were golden years, thanks to a coincidence of giants. Gardner was one of them, but his luck had turned, with still more injuries meaning he won only two races in 1991, finishing fifth. There was to be one final emotional win in his second home, England, in 1992.

Gardner retired from motorcycle racing, but continues to pursue a successful saloon car racing career in Australia and Japan, where his guts, bloody-mindedness and sheer determination make him a formidable competitor. Even if his feisty personality has mellowed somewhat.

Gardner came to prominence racing in England, and his aggressive style made him hugely popular. Here he shows his fans some speed in 1991. (Phil Masters)

Gardner joined up with ex-Spencer ex-Lawson tuner Erv Kanemoto in 1992, but injury spoiled his final season, except for an emotional final victory in Britain. (Henk Keulemans)

Wayne **Rainey**

Born
23 October 1960
Los Angeles, USA

500cc WORLD CHAMPIONSHIPS
1990 – Yamaha (Seven wins: Japanese GP, USA GP, Italian GP, Yugoslav GP, Belgian GP, Swedish GP, Czech GP)

1991 – Yamaha (Six wins: Australian GP, USA GP, European GP, French GP, San Marino GP, Czech GP)

1992 – Yamaha (Three wins: European GP, French GP, Brazilian GP)

Total 500cc GP wins: 24

Beach Boy looks and a casual Californian manner couldn't disguise the depth of a commitment that became an obsession for Wayne Rainey. (Henk Keulemans)

From sun-kissed California, with the looks of a surfer and the dedication of a monk, Wayne Rainey came into GP racing on the coat-tails of Kenny Roberts. He was set to outstrip his former mentor in 1993, when he'd fought back from the doldrums to claim a crucial late-season points lead. It would have been Rainey's fourth 500-class championship in a row, a feat at that time achieved only by Hailwood and Agostini.

Rainey takes comfort in the fact that the crash which ended his career happened when he was in the lead of the race and the championship, and had the throttle open. The injury was out of all proportion: thrown awkwardly into the gravel trap outside the first right-hand corner at his favourite circuit, Misano in Italy, 32-year-old Rainey broke his back so badly that he was lucky to survive, paralysed from the chest down.

Golden genius who could never be satisfied

What followed next was an inspiration. Bereft so abruptly of his main reason for living, Rainey returned to the tracks as soon as possible, first as a nominal team manager as part of the Kenny Roberts Yamaha empire, but soon afterwards as owner in his own right – of the official factory Marlboro Yamaha team, for whom he had won and won. Unfortunately, this coincided with something of a downturn in Yamaha's technical fortunes, while Rainey spent four frustrating years quite unable to find a rider who could come close to the sort of standard he demanded. He retired from racing at the end of 1998.

The shortcomings of the riders were, in retrospect, not unexpected. Rainey was of course hugely naturally talented on a motorcycle. Dirt-track and Superbike experience were combined with that instinctive feel, but in a field of more-or-less equally gifted peers, talent alone is not enough. Rainey found his edge through diligence and dedication. Nobody worked harder at racing, proven by the fact that he won so many races and so many titles on a Yamaha that was neither the best nor the fastest bike. That much showed clearly after Rainey had gone. It won because Wayne had made it win.

Wayne was the eldest of three children born to a hard-working blue-collar family in Downey, one of the sprawling, nondescript suburbs of Los Angeles. His father Sandy had been a go-kart racer; now he confined himself to motorcycles, preparing dirt-trackers for various local riders, and also for his sons. As Wayne remembers it, use of the bikes was dependent on getting good grades, good reports, and all the chores done properly. At the same time, surrounded by kids going off the rails in the permissive new times, Sandy saw motorcycles as a way of occupying his sons, to keep them on the straight and narrow.

The family rode in the nearby Mojave Desert at weekends, and at the junior race meetings at a number of little tracks in the LA area –

Having Kenny Roberts as team owner, friend and mentor meant that Wayne Rainey – seen here with Roberts in Italy in 1989 – was never short of advice. (Henk Keulemans)

Three weeks after claiming his first win, 500 rookie Rainey was a major factor at Brno for this 1988 Czechoslovakian GP battle. They finished Gardner, Lawson, Rainey, 2.5 seconds apart, in his first time at the track. (Henk Keulemans)

sometimes three or more times a week. When he wasn't racing, Wayne would practise … round and round and round at some disused oil field, or waste land, or even in the massive storm-water culverts that cut across the Los Angeles bowl.

The little blond boy was in the right place at the right time. Down the road was legendary dirt-track tuner Shell Thuet's shop, where as a wide-eyed kid he met Grand National Champion Kenny Roberts. Of more immediate relevance was another kid he met at the tracks, a little older, fast, and wearing a chromed steel-shoe to die for. It was Eddie Lawson. Eddie was from the other side of the huge city, and although the age difference was enough to preclude close friendship at this stage, they obviously recognised some sort of kindred perfectionism, for they hooked up together anyway. Lawson was a step or two ahead; Rainey followed naturally in his footsteps. They were team-mates on Thuet's dirt-track Yamahas in 1978; in 1980 he substituted for the injured Lawson in Kawasaki's junior dirt-track team. It wasn't all easy – far from it. Rainey served his time as a dirt-tracker, one of those national championship carnie types who'd show up at state fairs and places with a Harley in the back, spread a little mayhem, race a few races, then truck off to the next one. He never did win a grand national dirt-track event, and it is one of his few regrets. 'The talent I had I should have been winning, but I just didn't have it figured out then,' he told me, after his retirement.

Road-racing was beckoning. Again, he was summoned by Kawasaki, as junior Superbike team-mate to Lawson in 1980, and by 1983 their top rider, Eddie, had gone off to the GPs. Rainey won the title that year, his first major championship. But instead of the expected rewards, Kawasaki completed its corporate decision, made at the end of the previous season, to withdraw from racing. Wayne's career was over too. Or so it seemed to

Rainey's reign as the dominant 500 rider is just beginning, with the first of three championships in 1990. (Phil Masters)

The Belgian GP was the ninth round of 1990. Rainey – here with Lawson (1), Doohan (9) and Schwantz (34) – claimed a fifth win. He was moving inexorably towards his first title. (Henk Keulemans)

the disillusioned champion … until he met up with Kenny Roberts. Freshly retired, also at a loose end, Roberts hastily put together a low-budget 250 GP team for Rainey and British rider Allan Carter, and the US Superbike champion was all of a sudden a GP racer.

Wayne showed plenty of talent that first season, claiming one lap record and one pole position, and a classic rostrum finish at Misano, which he loved because the series of increasingly fast left-handers on to the back straight allowed him to use his wheelspinning dirt-track techniques, even on a 250. But he was flummoxed by the dead-engine push starts used at that time, and was left on the line over and over again. Somewhat overwhelmed also by the sheer culture shock, he would look back on the year as an uncomfortable catastrophe.

Wayne went back to the USA for 1985, for part two of his career at home, and in 1986 he was signed up by Honda for the national Superbike team. That year he conceded overall victory by only two points to team-mate Fred Merkel after a mixed-up season. The next year, 1987, there was something new – a tall, arrogant kid from Texas, with a big motorhome and a fast factory Suzuki. His name was Kevin Schwantz, and together Rainey and Schwantz would define racing for almost the next ten years.

Their fearsome rivalry actually erupted in Britain, at an epic series of Easter Match Races. It continued all year in the USA, and it was desperate. 'He was the only guy I'd deliberately run into throughout my racing career, and he was the only guy who ever deliberately ran into me,' Rainey told me. At the end of it all, Rainey was again US Superbike champion.

The crowds, of course, loved it. This was the real thing – two superb

Rivals who inspired each other to greatness – Rainey heads career-long adversary Kevin Schwantz in 1990. Sometimes they hardly even saw the other riders.
(Henk Keulemans)

The Yamahas of Rainey (2), Lawson (1) and Sarron (3) take centre stage in Belgium in 1990. The race, in atrocious weather, was a crucial win for Rainey, with Schwantz (34) back in seventh. (Henk Keulemans)

talents, at each other's throats. The scene was set for a golden age of GP racing, as the pair came to Europe together in 1988. Rainey rode a Yamaha for Kenny Roberts, in the new big-bucks team he had put together with Lucky Strike (later Marlboro) sponsorship. Schwantz rode a factory Suzuki, in Pepsi and then Lucky Strike colours. At a time when standards in the 500 class were already on a high, the two almost made the show their own.

In their first season, Schwantz was the first to win a 500 GP – the opening round – Rainey had to wait until late in the year for his, but his consistency was already showing and he was third overall, with Schwantz eighth in spite of another win.

In 1989, Rainey was ready to challenge. Schwantz again won double the number of races (six to three), but Rainey's consistency meant he was a title candidate right up until the closing stages, when a crash at the Swedish GP handed a fourth championship to Lawson.

The Rainey years began straight afterwards, when the records show a trio of back-to-back titles. They make it look easy but each was a major achievement. He wasn't only racing the mercurially talented Schwantz, but also all comers, who at that time included Eddie Lawson, Wayne Gardner, John Kocinski, Randy Mamola, Christian Sarron and (winning his first GP in 1990) Mick Doohan. Each championship had its own character: 1990 was clear, with seven race wins to Schwantz's five. The next year saw him have to dig deep to fight off Doohan, who won three races and added 11 other rostrum finishes as racing's next giant found full maturity in his third GP season. Rainey had been up against it mid-year, fighting back with a powerful late-season charge.

Australia's GP had moved to the start of the year, and to Sydney's Eastern Creek circuit. Rainey claimed the track's first 500 win, in 1991. (Henk Keulemans)

Rainey broke away to lead the 1991 Spanish GP, but when he ran into tyre problems rising star Mick Doohan's Honda pegged the champion's Yamaha back. Doohan won, Rainey clung on to third. (Henk Keulemans)

In 1992, he needed a bit of luck against the ever-improving Doohan/Honda combination. Equipped with the landmark Big Bang engine Mick was surging ahead on points when he went a click too far in practice at Assen. He broke his right leg badly, and was out for the next three races. The week before, Wayne had also crashed, in practice for the German GP, and he had already withdrawn, too sore to ride, from that fateful Dutch race. Now, with a glimmer of hope, he returned renewed – fighting back was by now something of a speciality. In the end, with the still-feeble Doohan attempting a ghostly comeback, there were just four points in it. In Rainey's favour.

Rainey's last year was another exemplar of skill, courage and diligence. Yamaha had taken a wrong turning with chassis design. With pure guts Rainey won two races on it, but ironically that only delayed fixing the problem: where was the urgency if the bike was still a winner? By Assen, Schwantz – having at last discovered consistency – was drawing ahead and looking like a champion. Rainey, 28 points behind and getting desperate, had one last card to play, bolting his factory motor into an old production-version Roc frame. It was enough to turn the tide.

Over the next four races Rainey won twice and was on the rostrum for the other two; Schwantz was third, second and fifth, but knocked off like a skittle by Doohan and failed to score in the British GP. By the time they got to Misano for the 12th of 14 rounds, Rainey had taken over the points lead, and Kevin was hurting. Rainey's crash put Schwantz in front once again.

Rainey conceded gracefully to his once-hated rival. Over the years the two had gained mutual respect and even warmth towards one another. Better that Kevin should have what he could no longer take, than anybody

Misano was a favourite track, and in 1991 Rainey led the charge into the first corner from Doohan (Honda), Kocinski and Didier de Radigues (Suzuki) – but more tyre trouble dropped him to tenth at the finish and Doohan extended his points lead. (Henk Keulemans)

By 1993, Schwantz and Rainey had added a growing respect to their fierce relationship. Here, Schwantz has narrowly won the Spanish GP. Rainey will close the gap and regain the points lead as the year wears on – but disaster was waiting. (Henk Keulemans)

In 1992, title rivals Rainey and Doohan both suffered injury. Wayne, here at the Hungarian GP, came back sooner and stronger for a third straight championship. (Henk Keulemans)

else, to end the era. It also brought to a close the chapter of American domination that had begun with Roberts 15 years before.

Rainey brought something else with him to racing – an old-fashioned kind of courtesy and decency; a respectful way of dealing with others that in turn engendered respect. It is hard to find a bad word about Wayne, among his rivals, team-mates, colleagues and acquaintances. The public never saw the other side – the alter ego he nicknamed Mr Buzzy, who would terrorise expensive restaurants all around Europe after another race win, turning haute cuisine into food-fight missiles, and antique tapestries into dishcloths.

Mr Buzzy was another reflection of a man whose drive to win was never satisfied, and who found disappointment at each world title, because he always expected something so hard to achieve would automatically bring proportionate satisfaction. It never did, and each time he was compelled to try and do it again, perhaps to find out why.

Even after his career was over, the demons did not let Rainey rest – but he had a new ally. His near-death experience at Misano had powerfully re-awakened a latent religious faith and as – over the next two or three years – he struggled to come to terms with the profound changes to his life, he drew strength from a deep and supportive belief.

Rainey is now happily distanced from racing. He spends time with his wife Shae and son Rex at their home overlooking Laguna Seca raceway outside Monterey, and on his powerful pleasure boat at Lake Tahoe in the Sierra Nevada. When he is not racing Eddie Lawson in a go-kart, a hand-control model specially built for him by his old friend, he likes to help coach Rex's baseball team at primary school.

Rainey's last ride – on the throttle and in the lead, from Yamaha team-mate Luca Cadalora, Schwantz and the rest of the field. (Henk Keulemans)

Less than a year after his terminal crash, Rainey was back in the grand prix pits as a team manager, alongside his former mentor Kenny Roberts. (Henk Keulemans)

Kevin Schwantz

Born
19 June 1964
Paige, Texas, USA

500cc WORLD CHAMPIONSHIP
1993 – Suzuki (Four wins: Australian GP, Spanish GP, Austrian GP, Dutch TT)

Total 500cc GP wins: *25*

Long tall Texan – Kevin Schwantz was better at winning races than championships, but his talent was rewarded in the end.
(Henk Keulemans)

It goes without saying that to win in racing you need plenty of talent. Kevin Schwantz is the proof that even with the most exceptional ability, championships don't come easily. For five years, from his full-time début in 1988 until 1992, Schwantz was almost always the man most likely to win any given race. The championship remained elusive, however, until the sixth year – and even then, he needed a bit of help.

In the meantime, Schwantz had to take his satisfaction from wins, pole positions and lap records. His career-long deadly rival, his inspiration, and now his friend, Wayne Rainey took most of the titles.

Schwantz's career-long Suzuki was seldom the best bike, but in his hands it was often unbeatable. Rainey would remark that Kevin could make a motorcycle do things it just wasn't meant to do. Unless, of course, he crashed.

Sixth time lucky for this fragile giant

Actually, that's a little unfair. Schwantz did fall off plenty, and almost always very visibly – usually in the lead. But his erratic results were not always his fault. And he seemed physically fragile, racking up wrist fractures and the like in crashes from which others might have escaped unscathed (once even while falling from a mountain bike). He would invariably go racing again as soon as it was remotely possible … barely waiting for the anaesthetic to wear off. This defining habit turned on him in later life. His wrists were permanently weakened and misshapen; his determination always to race rather than recover is now his only regret.

There were plenty of people to encourage this wilful streak. At Assen in

Schwantz and Suzuki engineer 'Mitsi' Okamoto in Japan in 1987. Kevin rewarded the factory with a fine win in the first race of his first full season. (Henk Keulemans)

Schwantz won two races in his début season, and already looked comfortable wearing a laurel wreath. (Phil Masters)

1994 he fractured his left wrist once again but raced two days later to a heroic fifth, finishing in agony, the cocktail of courage and strong painkillers all used up. I recall watching, admiration mixed with horror, as GP medic Dr Costa dropped to one knee next to the exhausted rider, a living tribute to his fix-'em-up medical code, and said: 'I love you!'

An exaggerated reputation? Take for example his second year as a full-time GP rider, 1989. The title was a bitter struggle between two masters of consistency, Lawson and Rainey. Schwantz said later that it should have been his. That year, out of 15 races he won six to Lawson's four and Rainey's three. He started from pole position nine times, and came away with eight new lap records. And in fact only fell off twice – once at Phillip Island, once while miles in the lead at Jerez. The other three no-scores were machine failures. Yet he finished only fourth, outpointed also by Frenchman Christian Sarron. 'That kind of set the pattern for me.'

The Schwantzes were a motorcycle family. Kevin was playbiking as a spindly kid, and took his racing number 34 from his dirt-tracking uncle Darryl Hurst (a 1975 AMA national winner). By nine, he was competing in trials and motocross. Uniquely among the top US riders of his generation, he never took to the dirt-track ovals. Then he discovered road-racing. Here he could exploit his extraordinarily athletic motorcycling skill – without getting dirty. Tarmac was his true métier. And Schwantz a true meteor.

Kevin brought with him a blend of trials-rider delicacy and motocross gung-ho. And he was brilliant. Drafted straight into the official factory Yoshimura Suzuki team in 1986, he chased winner Fred Merkel for the title all year. He and Merkel had been the main event at the annual Trans-Atlantic Match races in England, and Kevin also raced in three GPs – the first at Assen. He was fast in his first two-stroke race, but fell off three times. That certainly got him noticed.

Firmly from Texas, the opposite side of America from the LA Crucible, Kevin was never in the same loop as the Californian crowd. This was a good kick-off point for a state of bristling enmity with the rival who would define his glittering career. 'I guess I started off not liking Wayne Rainey because I wasn't meant to like him,' said Schwantz later. The feelings, and the inspiration, went both ways, and when they arrived simultaneously in the 500 class it was to begin a golden era.

They first met in 1987, with another Trans-Atlantic curtain raiser of fearsome intensity. The battle went on throughout the AMA season

Schwantz, Rainey, Doohan, Sarron and Lawson on the Belgian start line in 1989. Rain and a rules muddle eventually saw Lawson awarded the win, Schwantz second, the shambolic race carrying only half points. (Henk Keulemans)

Schwantz had a cavalier riding style all of his own. It brought him 25 wins. (Henk Keulemans)

(typically, Schwantz won more races, Rainey won the crown). In 1988 they were in the 500 class. Schwantz signalled his arrival with a superlative first-race win in Japan, defeating not only Rainey, but also Gardner and Lawson. Blatant genius – and he continued in the same vein, wearing his talent as casually as his urban cowboy clothes, and riding every race like there was no tomorrow.

In 1989 he was fourth; in 1990, he was equal on five wins apiece with Rainey but lagging on points when they arrived in Sweden for the 12th of 15 rounds. Then Kevin started to crash again. Wayne was champion. Kevin had equalled his five wins with five race falls.

Schwantz may have been courageous to the point of foolhardiness. But he wasn't stupid. Having failed in an attempt to switch to Yamaha, he brought a new philosophy to 1991. No more win or crash, no more heroics to make the machine do the impossible. Go for the best places instead. He still won five times – once with a long-remembered outbraking move on Rainey at Hockenheim – but with radically improved consistency. He had two no-scores, and only once because he'd crashed. Rainey and Doohan were stronger, but this was a new Schwantz.

In 1992, Mick Doohan and Honda's new Big Bang rewrote the rules. Schwantz was the first to break the Australian's spell, and when they reached that fateful Assen race, where Doohan broke his leg, Schwantz was ahead of eventual winner Rainey. He was leading the race too, when he was skittled by Lawson's Cagiva. He broke his left arm and dislocated his left hip. Three weeks later, his arm in a cast, he was back racing again in Hungary, finishing fourth. In the end, his worst season so far brought just

Schwantz in 1990. Being a superstar is an exhausting business, and his popularity would continue to grow with each fresh lap record or race win.
(Henk Keulemans)

Schwantz lets it all hang out at Laguna Seca in 1989. He finished second to Rainey as they relived their home-circuit rivalry.
(Phil Masters)

the one win, and fourth place overall. And Rainey won the title again.

All through his career, Schwantz had sparkled and flagged alternately, up against the obdurate Rainey. Each inspired and elevated the other. During qualifying, Schwantz was only ever interested in Rainey's lap time. An advantage either way of only one or two hundredths of a second could mean the difference between elation and despair. Rainey always saw the big picture. For Schwantz, it was race by race. It was while he was lying in hospital after the Assen crash that he realised that in spite of his new approach, in spite of being willing to accept defeat when necessary, race by race wasn't working.

His championship season of 1993 was almost flawless. He was a different rider, on a Suzuki having a good year. Always first out in practice, with a new, more methodical approach, he could still deploy the same inspiration on the track when he had to. But now he was focused on the next races as well. He won four of the first nine to Rainey's three. More significantly he had been in the top three at every race.

He arrived at the British GP 23 points ahead of Rainey and was expected to win from pole position – only for that notorious first-lap prang when Doohan knocked him and team-mate Alex Barros flying. Rainey, seeing double after a heavy practice crash, finished second in the depleted race; the points gap closed to just three.

What really spoiled it for Schwantz was the lingering effect of his frequent wrist injuries, which led to the notorious Racer's Wrist, or carpal tunnel syndrome. This got rapidly worse as the year wore on, so by race end his throttle hand was weak and numb. A further fracture in England made it worse still. From now on, he was riding hurt, and would require

Assen was a special track for Schwantz, and he still holds the lap record. Here in 1991 he celebrates defeating Rainey at the classic Dutch circuit. (Henk Keulemans)

Donington Park in 1992, and Schwantz and Rainey lead the British Grand Prix. A freak crash on spilled oil cost Schwantz any chance of scoring points. (Henk Keulemans)

surgery at the year's end. And Rainey won the next race at Brno to take over the title lead.

The rest is tragic history. Kevin didn't win another race that year, and his closing rides were pitiful – he was even at times using his left hand to hold the throttle on the straights. But he had done enough earlier in the year to claim at last the crown that had seemed to have slipped from his fingers yet again.

It may be force of circumstance, but Kevin's own view on his lack of title success compared with his win rate seems completely sincere. 'For some reason, it didn't burn me up. Winning titles was what I wanted, but at the same time I was still proving the point that I could be the fastest guy out there. I could win, win, win – ah shit. So I made a mistake, and it cost me the championship.'

More costly was the loss of his rival, and his inspiration. Mentally as well as physically weakened, Schwantz won two more races the next year to bring his total to 25; and came back again in 1995. By now, however, he was in some mental anguish. After a lacklustre sixth in the rain at Suzuka – conditions in which he'd previously reigned supreme – he spoke for hours on the flight home with his old rival Rainey, now a wheelchair-bound team manager. He went AWOL for a while, and returned mid-season only, in an emotional ceremony, to announce his retirement. His racing number 34 was retired with him – an unprecedented move. It was the end of an era.

Schwantz tried his hand next at NASCAR oval-track racing but left after surviving a heavy crash. Today he still works with Suzuki's racing team in the USA, and has recently opened a road-racing school at Road Atlanta, Georgia.

Schwantz at Le Mans in 1994 – his last full season brought hardship along with two more wins.
(Henk Keulemans)

How popular was Kevin Schwantz? The impromptu banner says it all.
(Henk Keulemans)

Mick**Doohan**

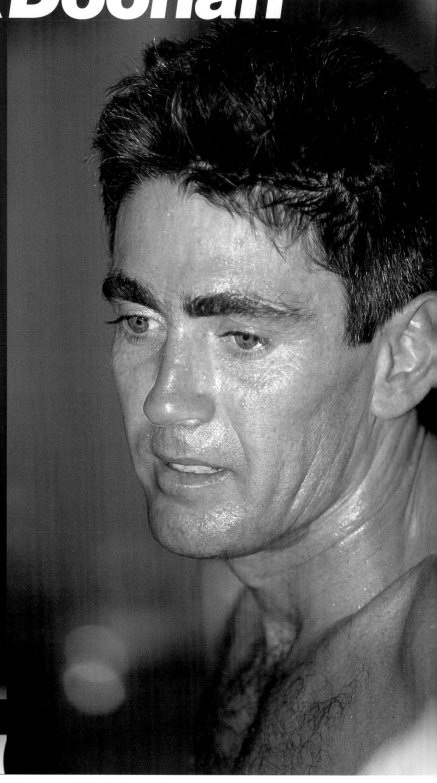

Born
4 June 1965
Brisbane, Australia

500cc WORLD CHAMPIONSHIPS

1994 – Honda (Nine wins: Malaysian GP, Spanish GP, Austrian GP, German GP, Dutch TT, Italian GP, French GP, Czech Republic GP, Argentine GP)

1995 – Honda (Seven wins: Australian GP, Malaysian GP, Italian GP, Dutch TT, French GP, British GP, Argentine GP)

1996 – Honda (Eight wins: Indonesian GP, Spanish GP, Italian GP, French GP, Dutch GP, British GP, Imola GP, Rio GP)

1997 – Honda (Twelve wins: Malaysian GP, Japanese GP, Italian GP, Austrian GP, French GP, Dutch TT, Imola GP, German GP, Rio GP, British GP, Czech Republic GP, Catalunyan GP)

1998 – Honda (Eight wins: Malaysian GP, Italian GP, Dutch TT, German GP, Imola GP, Catalunyan GP, Australian GP, Argentine GP)

Total 500cc GP wins: 54

All the agony and effort was worth it – five times

People have different views on why Mick Doohan was so dominant, how after an era of extreme competitiveness one man was able to rise so far clear of the rest. Riders from the previous era will point out that he achieved his success after they had retired. Doohan will counter that he beat them too, when they were there. Then there are those who try to compare Doohan with Agostini – the only rider with more decorations and race wins. The Doohan camp will counter that for many of his titles Ago was virtually unopposed.

Both views are valid. In the end Doohan's career is a perfect illustration of the basic truth that the champion is the one who beats the people he has to beat, the rivals of the time. He can do no more. And if they are all miles behind him, to the point that the racing becomes dull? Then in Doohan's own pithy comment: 'What do you want me to do – slow down?'

There were never any signs that Doohan would not have been equal to much tougher opposition. He certainly was never a rider who would only go just fast enough. Riding often as not marvellously alone, so far in front of the rest that they might as well have stayed home, he kept on pushing to claim one pole position and one lap record after another. Some of his race average times had yet to be beaten two years after he was forcibly removed by injury in 1999.

Doohan was the youngest of three sons from Brisbane. It was his eldest brother Colin who first got bitten by motorcycling mania. Father Colin Senior had himself ridden, and soon the whole family were playing on two wheels, eight-year-old Mick at the bottom of the heap. Before long, Colin had opened a motorbike shop, and family and friends took regular outings to the nearby Nudgee Dump, where they could practise to their hearts' content. There were short-track and motocross races galore – like the Americans, Mick was the beneficiary of the baby-bike boom of the Seventies.

Family catastrophe came when Mick was just 11, when Colin Senior died. It hit Mick hard. Over the next years he drifted in and out of motorcycles, and admits to having been a difficult, wilful teenager.

By 19, Mick was a daring road rider. A bit too daring, and when he turned up yet again at the local bike breaker to fix his crashed 350 Yamaha (actually a mate had pranged it this time) the shop owner – a racing benefactor who believed young hooligans were better off the public roads and on the track – repaired it free, on condition Mick would enter a race the next weekend at Surfer's Paradise circuit. The year was 1984, and Mick was about to get on an express train.

He'd also be picked up by a bike-loving bunch of drinking partners who went racing for the fun of it. Mick fitted in well with the gang, who put camouflage overalls over his leathers, painted the bike (a Yamaha RD500) likewise, and had paddock HQ in an army tent covered with netting.

Mick was fast – on the 500, as well as various 250 and 750 production bikes – winning one out of every two races. By 1987 he was in the Australian big time, the national Superbike championships, up against some high-class opposition. He first rode the Marlboro Yamaha machine that year, and in 1988 was teamed with Mike Dowson in a formidable double act. He also ran in four World Superbike events in 1988, and won three of them.

GP racing didn't merely beckon. Eighteen months after racing a 250

Sustained excellence and serial dominance were not enough to satisfy the burning hunger of Australian hero Mick Doohan. By 1997, he was looking all of his 32 years. (Henk Keulemans)

production bike, Doohan was sought after by the two top 500 teams. He tested a Yamaha but, looking at the other up-and-coming talent already riding the V4s, decided he might be better taking the other offer. It was from Honda, at that time a smaller player, where he joined 1987 champion Wayne Gardner.

I remember the first time I saw Doohan ride a 500, at Suzuka for the opening round of 1989. He came flying over the hill behind the pits with the rear wheel spinning, in a slide at least as wild as any of the established stars. Uniquely, he appeared in no way fazed by the awesome power and mad responses of a 500. He looked born to be champion. If he could survive that long. The first year was hard – fighting an ill-handling bike, under the shadow of Gardner. And the crashes. From race two, Mick was riding with stoical courage, on a bike he later admitted was frankly frightening, with two fingers on his left hand ground down to the bone. Scorning skin grafts, he would anoint the ghastly open wound with jelly, don a surgical glove, put on his racing gloves and go out again. 'I'm not a pain-killer type of person,' he would later say, on many occasions.

By the end of it, after breaking his hand and later his arm once again, he was a different rider – he had faced the terror of a modern 500, and come out the other side determined to get the better of it. The party animal turned teetotal – just one side of a fearsome new dedication that was to grind the opposition to dust.

Mick had another asset. The ruling classes – Rainey, Lawson, Gardner and Schwantz – were masters of rear-wheel steering, using a relatively low corner speed and a blistering wheelspinning exit speed. Doohan added something new: fast entry and mid-corner speed. Having joined the top

Doohan leads team-mate Gardner at Laguna Seca, 1990. The Australian pair were better rivals than they were colleagues.
(Henk Keulemans)

The 1991 season began with a superb close race at Suzuka in Japan. At the finish, Schwantz (34) led Doohan, Rainey and John Kocinski over the line, the group all within almost half a second.
(Henk Keulemans)

level, he now pushed it higher – though his first race win (in Hungary) came only in his second season.

Mick was much sought after. He came close to joining Suzuki, using primitive subterfuge to back out of the deal at the last moment. But he stayed with Honda, and through the year outpointed Gardner, and confirmed himself as HRC's top man. Already his skill at bike development, working hand in glove with crew chief and fellow Australian Jerry Burgess, was paying off. Mick and Jerry knew what worked, and nobody was as forceful as Doohan at resisting the HRC engineers' constant pressure to change it. Indeed, the 1992 NSR was to remain basically unchanged beyond the end of his career, much to his and eventually his successors' benefit.

In 1992 the final piece of the mechanical jigsaw was put into place: the 'Big Bang' close-firing-order engine. Doohan won the first four races – Japan, Australia, Malaysia and Jerez – and was second to Schwantz at Mugello, with tyre trouble. At the next race in Catalunya, pulling inexorably clear on points, he was outfoxed by an increasingly desperate Rainey. But in his haste the American was becoming reckless, and a second crash in Germany put him out there and at the next round at Assen. Doohan was 57 points clear of an absent rival at the mid-point of the year. It looked like a downhill cruise.

It all came undone at the Dutch track. Mick crashed in qualifying and broke his right leg below the knee. The fracture was relatively straightforward, but Mick blames botched treatment at the Assen hospital for almost losing his leg, and a nightmare to follow that left him with a permanent and serious limp. Doohan was whisked to Dr Costa's clinic in

In 1992 Honda's Big Bang engine came along, and Mick's partnership with crew chief Jerry Burgess really started to gel. But there were troubles ahead. (Henk Keulemans)

Fully recovered, fully determined, Doohan resumed his steamroller progress in 1994, and didn't stop for the next five years.
(Henk Keulemans)

Italy where the right leg was saved only by sewing it to his left leg for two weeks to revive the circulation. By the time he could walk again, Doohan was a ghost of his former self, and though he made a miraculous semi-crippled return two months later for the last two races, at Brazil and South Africa, he was in no way able to stop Rainey from taking his third and final title at the last race.

Doohan had to dig deep again in 1993. He was physically weak – a pre-season crash, caused by mechanical failure, had left him with a broken wrist and the leg even worse. It bent like a banana, leading to further remedial surgery that would last for several years. Another rider to use the rear brake to the full, but now unable to operate the pedal with his ruined right leg, he pioneered a thumb-operated extra lever on the left handlebar – a measure of his determination to get back on full form. At the same time, he was plagued with uncertainty. 'If I'd won the title in 1992 I'd probably have given up racing,' he said later.

Nor was the bike to Mick's liking. His absence for much of the previous year had allowed the engineers to take off on typical HRC flights of fancy – including a nearly-ready fuel injection system. The omens were not good.

Doohan added just one race win that year, finishing fourth overall, below even his inexperienced compatriot, team-mate and friend Daryl Beattie. He completed the physical self-destruction with a shoulder broken from a last-round crash. It was the year also that Rainey's career ended in catastrophe, and Schwantz took the title. Mick ended it with more surgery to his leg, and his first (but not last) encounter with the gruesome Ilizarov frame, an adjustable external fixing that he would re-tension every day to bend the bones straight again.

All this agony, and all this effort, was now to be rewarded however. Rainey was out of 500 racing, Gardner had also gone, and Lawson;

The new king, and those who sought his throne – Schwantz was reigning champion, but a relaxed Doohan was forging ahead. The two giants exchange insults with Australian Daryl Beattie and Brazilian Alex Barros. (Henk Keulemans)

In his third championship year, 1996, Mick's closest opposition usually came from team-mate Alex Criville. The older rider easily kept the upper hand. (Henk Keulemans)

Schwantz was carrying injuries. Even if it had been otherwise, it is hard to predict that the outcome would have been any different. For by 1994 Mick had become, apparently, unbeatable.

During his first title season, Doohan won nine out of 14 races and the championship with a record points score of 317 points (the previous record had been Rainey's 255 in 1990). The next-best scorer, 125 and double 250 champion Luca Cadalora, had just 174. This is as good as any a measure of Doohan's devastating superiority.

In 1995 Beattie ran him a bit closer, but more by consistency than brilliance, winning twice to Doohan's seven times. It was somewhat dour stuff, and though Doohan fumed that he'd been taken out of context when quoted as saying 'racing is as boring as shit now', he wasn't far from the truth. Not surprisingly, he resented getting the blame.

Over the next three years, Doohan reigned supreme. He seemed to take it a little easier on himself (there was quite a lot of room for that), and now and then somebody would catch up and even beat him. Not often, and never by far. More of the time Doohan would win by miles, adding steadily to his total of 500-class victories – eight in 1996, a dizzying 12 in 1997, and eight more in 1998. By the end of that year he had recorded 54 race wins, second only to Agostini on 68. Ago had taken 11 years from his first win to his last, Doohan just nine, though admittedly with many more races each year.

There were to be no more. Mick was beaten in the opening two rounds of the 1999 season – in Malaysia he had handling problems and was a close fourth, behind team-mate and frequent shadow Alex Criville as Kenny Roberts Junior claimed his first GP win. In Japan he was second to Roberts in a wet race, the new kid manfully fending off his attack. Had he met his nemesis? Probably not, but this was never to be proven.

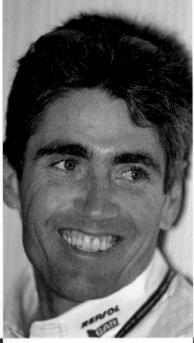

In his fifth year of world domination, Doohan ruled by right, and challengers were few.
(Henk Keulemans)

The Catalunya circuit outside Barcelona gave Carlos Checa his first GP win. Here the Hondas of Alex Criville (4), Mick Doohan and Luca Cadalora dispute second. Doohan took it. (Henk Keulemans)

At the next round at Jerez, in one momentary lapse Doohan touched a wet white line with his rear wheel. Spat off at 135mph, he was thrown into a trackside hoarding, and sustained multiple injuries – breaking his right leg again, as well as his left wrist and right shoulder. He put a brave face on it, promising to be back, but the truth was that the leg was bad enough, and he had suffered nerve damage with the shoulder injury. He would never race again.

Doohan was so much the giant of his time that he inevitably faced criticism. Given his achievements, it seems a little unfair. Weak opposition? He made them so. The best bike? He made it so. And to be fair, as well as the earlier Suzuki flirtation, Mick came close to signing also for Yamaha at the end of 1995. It was only botched negotiations from their side that spoiled what might have been an even better party.

Doohan blazed a new trail in racing, in so many ways. He certainly pioneered the highest level of earnings ever. And he did it all with a determination and dedication that set new standards in a world of excellence. He always said that the championship itself was not the goal – 'just a number 1 that you put on your bike, and you can't even see it when you're riding. What drives me is the instant gratification of winning races.' His record of 12 wins in a season is one more than that of Agostini. The man who breaks it will be another cast in the same mould as the two greatest champions of the 500 class.

After the crash Doohan continued to live in Monaco, rejoined by Selina and their new daughter Allexis. He worked for HRC as general racing manager, and – when he had finally come to terms with his enforced premature retirement – eased up on himself enough to show some glimpses of the much more cheerful young man he had left behind in his drive for perfection.

It had been a hell of a ride.

Doohan's final crash, early in 1999, didn't quench his desire to ride – and he was still talking about coming back when he visited the mid-season Dutch TT on crutches. His injuries, however, were too severe. (Henk Keulemans)

After retirement as a rider, Doohan stayed active as Honda's General Manager of Racing. And having Rossi as one of his charges kept him smiling. (Henk Keulemans)

Alex Criville

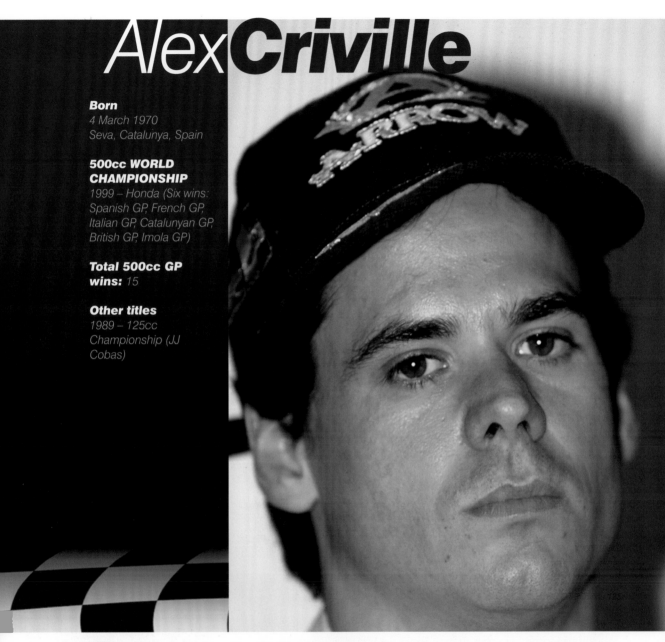

Born
4 March 1970
Seva, Catalunya, Spain

500cc WORLD CHAMPIONSHIP
1999 – Honda (Six wins: Spanish GP, French GP, Italian GP, Catalunyan GP, British GP, Imola GP)

Total 500cc GP wins: 15

Other titles
1989 – 125cc Championship (JJ Cobas)

Alex Criville rewarded the patient support of his home country in 1999, taking over where Doohan had left off on the dominant Repsol Honda.
(Henk Keulemans)

The quiet conquistador

Alex Criville is not a typical World Champion. Modest and retiring, with a somewhat similar riding style, he seems to fit his post-championship role better – that of a one-time star sustained by the seemingly endless loyalty of his fans and sponsors, and the occasional fast lap or good result. Yet the quiet one from the hills outside Barcelona has won not only the 500 championship, but also the 125 title in 1989, when he was the youngest person ever to do so.

Alex might then have slipped into relative obscurity, but for his low-key determination, and some high-level patronage. He moved to the 250 class where his performance over the next two years was undistinguished. But to those in the know he had a talent for accurate riding, as well as a growing maturity. Hired by a new team owner, retired

Criville was hungry to win in Spain in 1996, but Doohan was having none of it. They clashed in the last hairpin, and the Spaniard came off second best. (Henk Keulemans)

The Repsol Honda Armada – Criville and Doohan in close formation in 1996. (Henk Keulemans)

Criville pulls the fast train in 1998, ahead of Doohan, Barros and Cadalora. He won two races that season. (Henk Keulemans)

double 250 champion Sito Pons, and with top tuner Antonio Cobas (his machine manufacturer in the 125 class), Alex was taken into the 500 class in 1992. It was his career-long goal. A first-season win at Assen was something of a fluke, with all the top guns out either before or during the race. Even so, Alex gradually and unobtrusively achieved the keenly sought-after role of Spain's top rider, at a time when it really mattered. The sport was growing fast in Spain, with the Spanish company Dorna soon to take over the running of the GPs, and big sponsors crowding to get in on the act.

Alex rode for Pons for two years, when he was able to be confident of well-funded backing and good motorcycles. Then came Repsol, with a grand plan to take over the then unsponsored official factory Honda team, left high and dry by the withdrawal of Rothmans, and to put a Spanish rider on the bike. Criville was the man for the top job, and from now on he could also be sure of an even higher profile and bigger fan base, as his face gazed contemplatively down from roadside advertising hoardings and at service station forecourts.

Was it his good luck to be Mick Doohan's team-mate? Or the other way round? That's a tough call. Mick, Honda's incumbent champion, was fully aware of the dictum that your team-mate is the first person you have to beat, and while he didn't seem to have much trouble doing that to the younger and less experienced rider, it never hurt to reinforce the pecking order. Criville sat in the other corner of the pit almost timidly as Doohan swept all before him, on and off the track.

But Criville was paying attention to various aspects – not just what a Honda NSR could be made to do and how to set it up to do that, but also how to live under pressure. 'I learned a lot of things from Mick,' he told me during his title year. 'I gained a lot of experience, fighting with him on the track. And the way he works. Mick sometimes doesn't change the bike, but he works very hard on himself, pushing very hard from the first day. You must look for the extra speed in yourself. I learned that from Mick.' But what was it like, working with such a reluctant teacher? 'Our relationship is … professional. It is difficult to be friends, when you are at the track.'

Not surprising, because Doohan did not conceal his contempt for what was, after all, a reasonable tactic under the circumstances. Where Mick led, still improving over the years, Criville was eventually able to follow. And to follow so closely, in the case of the 1996 Czech Republic GP at Brno, that he managed to nip past on the sprint to the line to defeat his illustrious team-mate by two thousandths of a second.

Mick was angry, perhaps with his own complacency for letting it happen. It was a sign that Criville was ready, however, whenever Mick wasn't going to be there. Which finally happened for the Spaniard in 1999. Doohan crashed out in only the third round – leaving Criville undisputed head man at the Honda factory team.

Nobody should underestimate the title he won. When Doohan fell, Roberts was ahead on points, having won the first two rounds in spite of Doohan's presence, and Criville had to act fast to exert his authority. This he did by winning at that Jerez round, while Roberts trailed in 13th with his bike damaged after a collision with team-mate Aoki on the first lap. Perhaps the turning point was two weeks later, however, at Paul Ricard in France. Criville's Honda was clearly superior, and Roberts crashed in his desperate attempts to keep up. Criville won again two weeks later in Italy, once more in Barcelona, and though it was his turn

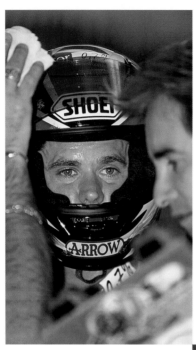

Alex in 1999 with crew chief Gilles Bigot – together they held off a strong challenge from Kenny Roberts. (Henk Keulemans)

Alex's first win of 1999 came at home in Jerez – holding a persistent Max Biaggi's Yamaha at bay to the flag. (Henk Keulemans)

National pride went both ways with Alex Criville in his championship year. (Henk Keulemans)

to crash out at Assen, he won again in Britain, and once more, at Imola, two more races down the road. But it was that mid-season stretch that gave him the cushion he needed for the title, even though by year's end he was exhausted, and had kept Roberts's hopes alive until the second-last race, after breaking bones in his wrist in a practice crash for the Australian GP.

As Spain's first 500 champion, he was fêted tirelessly upon his return. It was hardly surprising, in among the public appearances and VIP treatment, that the winter proved as exhausting as the preceding summer. Criville suffered a collapse at pre-season testing with a mystery virus taking the blame – though some suspected more serious problems. Certainly he reverted to his earlier form, winning just once (at Le Mans) during his season as champion, and seeming to suffer as much from a want of direction and motivation as anything else. Perhaps his good year had been a single legacy, from Doohan, which ended as the Australian's influence faded?

Or was it that, his hunger satisfied, it all became a bit too much of a fuss for this modest racer?

In 2000, Criville and his Repsol Honda team-mates had difficulty in finding the right settings for their new NSR. (Henk Keulemans)

Kenny **Roberts Jnr**

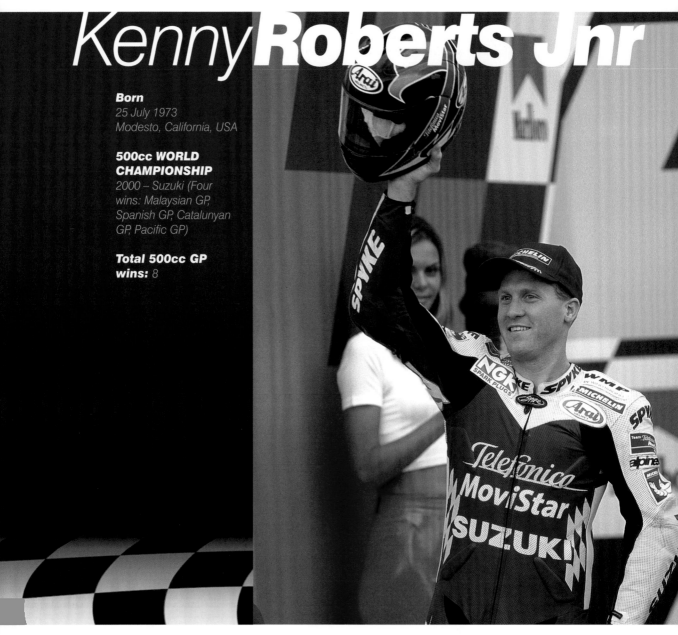

Born
25 July 1973
Modesto, California, USA

500cc WORLD CHAMPIONSHIP
2000 – Suzuki (Four wins: Malaysian GP, Spanish GP, Catalunyan GP, Pacific GP)

Total 500cc GP wins: 8

Kenny Roberts Junior combined privilege, talent and determination to repeat his father's world-beating feat.
(Henk Keulemans)

Like father, like son? In the record books, yes – but only once in the 500 class. Kenny Roberts Junior made history in 2000 when he took the Suzuki to its first World Championship since Schwantz seven years before, the first son of a previous title-holder to do so. The convincing and hard-ridden win followed a strong début year on the same bike; and showed Kenny's strengths not only as a consistent and accurate rider, but also as a tough fighter. And a worthy heir to the title King Kenny.

The next year was very different. Kenny's results slumped, and the fight seemed to have gone out of him. He complained that his machine was basically unimproved since the previous year, when he already had to ride the wheels off it, while the rivals had all got better. Apart from a single rostrum third place at Valencia in a wet-and-dry race (new team-mate Sete

He hadn't given up, he was just resting

Gibernau came first), he never did finish higher than sixth. Statistically it was the worst ever title defence since Masetti in 1953. In this way, he forfeited the chance to repeat his father's feat of back-to-back titles.

Given his confident strength previously, this was a puzzle. One answer lies in his father's record. Kenny Senior's reputation was founded on his determined, aggressive riding, but strongly tinged with his maverick role – a Yank against the world. Kenny Junior's entry to GP racing was very different, the way paved with a family team and factory bikes, even as a 500-class rookie. But Kenny Senior was also lauded as a thinking rider, who would decline to risk too much for victory when the equipment wasn't up to

In 1996 Junior was already in the 500 class on a Team Roberts Yamaha. He started well, but had to spend two years in waiting before he got another factory V4 racer. (Henk Keulemans)

Kenny came to GPs in 1994 in the 250 class. Some thought he had it easy – but he quietly got on with paying his dues. (Henk Keulemans)

the job. His son is the same way – only in his circumstances, it shows up rather more clearly.

Junior, or Little Kenny as he is known to the Modesto mob, was almost literally born to race. An infant in the paddocks while his father was winning three titles, he moved with his mother, sister and younger brother back to Modesto when the couple divorced, and grew up in a typical if well-heeled rural Californian suburban background – getting grades, playing sports hard, and meeting teenage sweetheart Rochelle, now his wife.

Little Kenny's other life was all bikes and racing, at dad's nearby ranch, handily equipped with acres of rough riding, masses of motorcycles … and an oval dirt-track. Here Kenny would ride for hours and days, and seldom

alone. His companions were not only his father, but the likes of Randy Mamola, Eddie Lawson, Wayne Rainey and many others, a roll call of American racing stars. 'Every weekend was like a grand prix to me,' he recalls. 'I always knew I could beat those guys one day.'

Kenny Senior insists he never pushed him into racing. Junior concurs. The decision was his own, at the age of 15, after watching Kocinski race at Willow Springs. 'I'd ridden with him, and I knew I could do that too, and hopefully a hell of a lot better,' he realised, and immediately called his dad with the not entirely welcome news that he had decided to become a professional racer.

Kenny Senior, racing's top team owner, was in a position to give the kid a silver path straight to the top. Once he was convinced of the depth of Junior's commitment, he did so. Inevitably, many (especially other riders) were jealous and quick to criticise. They failed to notice the effort Junior was putting in on his own account, and that while he was beaten in the US championships by Colin Edwards (Wayne's father, Sandy Rainey, was Junior's team chief), the kid was applying himself to the complexities of the art and science of racing. Steadily and smoothly, he was raising his game.

From the US championships and some dogfighting in Spain, Kenny came straight to the GPs in 1994, riding a Marlboro Yamaha 250 in a team owned by his father and run by Wayne Rainey in his come-back to racing the season after the crash that ended his riding career. And Kenny went and spoiled it all, breaking his arm in a pre-season training accident, and taking half the year to recover. Having already finished in the top ten as a wild card in the 1993 US GP, his best finish when he did return was sixth. His second season was more like a first, seeing new tracks and learning the

Kenny left his father's team to join Suzuki in 1999 – and started out by winning the first two races of the season. (Henk Keulemans)

Kenny's title-winning campaign brought him four race wins – but here, at Donington Park, he had to give best to rising star Valentino Rossi. (Henk Keulemans)

routines of GP racing. This time he did better, with a best of fourth, and eighth overall in a class dominated by Max Biaggi. Hardly enough, some said, to warrant a step straight up into Yamaha's factory 500 team, riding a coveted YZR500 V4 in Marlboro colours, for his father's huge Team Roberts. Again, Kenny got on with the business, qualifying on the front row at Brno, and claiming a best of fourth.

The 1997 season saw a huge change in the family fortunes, as Kenny Senior split with Yamaha and set up as a racing manufacturer in his own right. Junior went with him, to spend two years racing the Modenas three-cylinder lightweight motorcycle built by his father's company. Seldom good enough for more than low top-ten finishes, the Modenas did have the advantage of taking Junior out of the limelight – few other riders envied his bike now. He continued to improve as a racer, setting steady and ever-faster lap times, measuring himself against and then outriding some classy team-mates. He was also learning an awful lot about motorcycle dynamics, since the team weren't merely refining an existing design, but had started with a clean sheet of paper to create a brand new machine.

Kenny formed a crucial alliance with former rider and now dedicated racing engineer Warren Willing, a member of the tight-knit Team Roberts, led hands-on by Kenny Senior. When the chance came to move to Suzuki, to a V4 factory machine, during 1998, Junior turned as always to his father for advice. And he agreed the move offered more potential than staying on the Modenas. Just one thing though. 'If I went, he wanted Warren to go with me.'

Suzuki was recovering from a post-Schwantz slump, after sundry vicissitudes, especially with riders. They had lost momentum, and also

Roberts made the most of his chances in 2000, building up a solid points advantage from the start. By the time his rivals picked up momentum, it was too late. Here he powers on to second place in Portugal. (Henk Keulemans)

Close quarters and no prisoners taken – Kenny leads the 500cc brawl at Germany's tight Sachsenring circuit in 2000. (Henk Keulemans)

sponsorship. Now the factory had revitalised their machine, and Kenny and Warren both fitted perfectly in with their overall strategy to upgrade the team to match. The new pair hatched their own battle plan: one season to get the bike set to their liking, to achieve its fullest potential; the second to go for the championship.

That plan went wrong from the start. Kenny won the opening two rounds of 1999, in Malaysia and Japan, where he even outrode Mick Doohan in the wet, and he was leading the championship when they came to Europe. There Doohan's career came to an abrupt close.

Kenny won two more races that year, but a headstrong crash in France and a disintegrating tyre at the other end of the season in Australia meant that Alex Criville and Honda eventually won out.

Year Two did go to plan. Kenny put together an exemplary season – consistently tough and aggressive, intimidating the opposition and piling up four more wins among a set of strong finishes only interrupted once, when his engine seized and he crashed while leading on the first lap at Assen. By the end of that second Suzuki season, the strongest challenge came from class rookie Valentino Rossi, but Kenny had him covered too, underlining it by a convincing defeat of the Italian at Motegi.

'Kenny's worked real hard for this,' said his proud father. 'He's had to put up with a lot of bullshit along the way, that he's had it easy because of me. Now he's proved his ability to everybody.'

Curiously enough, Junior echoed the bullshit comment – but about his father being criticised for nepotism, illustrating a closeness of relationship that many find hard to understand. Kenny may (like all of them) race 'for myself', but he does so for and with his father's approval, and asks his advice every step of the way. 'Most times I do whatever he tells me, because he's pretty much always right,' he told me – meaning racing advice, and general advice. And there was never a question of Junior racing against his father's team: Senior was as much an ally to Suzuki as a rival, spending as much time in their garage as in his own Modenas team pit.

Kenny was perfectly clear in his own mind about the technical reasons for his very different performance in 2001. 'We have a severe engine deficit … too much engine braking, and an acceleration problem. It's something that we've had for a couple of years now, but we're not able to hide it any more,' he stormed after the third round at Jerez, where he'd finished seventh. This was largely a function of tyres. The better grip of the new-generation 16.5-inch rear had allowed the more powerful rival machines to make use of their extra power, while emphasising the Suzuki's relative shortcoming. Kenny tried hard for a couple more races, only to fall off in the rain at Mugello (one of many) and again in Catalunya, then he seemed to accept the inevitable, and settle back to await expected technical improvements from the smallest Japanese factory team.

Nobody who had seen him race the year before, or studied his progress over the years from platinum kid to very serious World Champion, could believe that this was the whole story. And soon after the end of a dismal and depressing year came promising news. Suzuki had put forward by a year their plan to introduce an all-new four-stroke racer for the new 990cc class – and Roberts would have a chance of a fresh start. It was a chance to prove that the first ever father-and-son champion hadn't given up. He was just resting.

Valentino Rossi

Born
16 February 1979
Urbino, Italy

500cc WORLD CHAMPIONSHIP
2001 – Honda (Eleven wins: Japanese GP, South African GP, Spanish GP, Catalunyan GP, British GP, Czech Republic GP, Portuguese GP, Pacific GP, Australian GP, Malaysian GP, Rio GP)

Total 500cc GP wins: 13

Other titles
1997 – 125cc World Championship (Aprilia)

1999 – 250cc World Championship (Aprilia)

Rossi took two years to dominate the 125s, another two for the 250s. Then he did the same again to become the last ever 500 champion.
(Henk Keulemans)

The last prize on offer from the 500 class was an object of great desire. Kenny Roberts Junior of course wanted to retain his crown, Max Biaggi to win his first; Yamaha to close the two-stroke era with the last as well as the first title; Loris Capirossi to add the 500 to his portfolio of 125 and 250 crowns, to become the only rider other than Phil Read to win this triple combination, in the last year it would be possible. Only one other rider was in a position to do this.

In 2001, however, the gods had another favourite in mind. A rider who could do no wrong. And so Valentino Rossi, born to greatness, continued the swathe he had cut through the 125 and 250 classes. One year to learn, one year to win. Just in time to close a chapter of history with a hatful of extra feathers in his cup – winner of Honda's 500th GP and their 150th

Fitting idol to wear the final crown

500-class GP. Plus the Suzuka Eight-Hour race. And the Phil Read hat trick that Capirossi had coveted.

And, of course, that last-ever championship bearing the magic numbers: 500.

The final season was a fitting epitaph to 52 years of 500cc Grand Prix racing. The Australian GP had the closest finish of all time – first place to ninth covered by just 2.8 seconds. And the winner – as at ten other races of the year – was Rossi, a flash of yellow on a Honda on the very edge of control, snatching victory from his deadly rival Biaggi by inches. During this epic 16-race season, Rossi claimed his 11 wins against the fiercest competition perhaps in the history of the class, smiling his rubber-lipped grin to an army of fans that was rapidly growing far beyond the narrow confines of bike racing.

Rossi fitted easily into the role of modern racing god. New-century man – full of fun and fashion and spontaneous laughter, an easy-going idol who at the age of 21 had already felt obliged to flee from his native Italian holiday coast, the pressure of idolatry too much to allow even a semblance of a normal life, to live instead in London's elegant Pall Mall.

Born to race? Rossi's father was Graziano, a dashing and colourful racer of the late Seventies, three times a GP winner whose career was cut short by injury. And the infant Valentino was a paddock cherub in his leather-clad father's arms, waking up in a caravan with two-stroke racers revving outside. Normal life.

Graziano and Rossi's mother Stefania split up soon afterwards, and the boy was raised by his mother in Urbino, close to the Rimini coast and to the Misano circuit. The family remained close, however, and he was often with his father. Quality time, as it turned out, because motorsport-mad Graziano soon had his son driving go-karts, and riding motorcycles from the age of five.

Valentino's early teens coincided with a boom in a wacky form of junior motorcycle racing – mini-moto. Kids crouched on pocket-sized bikes little

Rossi's 125 title came in 1997 – to an ever-smiling imp with an androgynous haircut. He was just 18. (Henk Keulemans)

Rossi, tucked in and styling in South Africa. (Gold and Goose)

larger than skateboards, knees splayed, raced hell for leather round the many go-kart tracks in Rimini, and at almost every seaside town. For Valentino, this apprenticeship not only whetted his appetite, but also served the same purpose as had the dirt-track ovals to a generation of American GP heroes. 'I learned to ride off the edge of the tyre, and to slide with the power and on my knees,' he explains.

By the age of 14, Rossi had been talent-spotted by Aprilia racing boss Carlo Pernat. He cut his teeth in the 125 production class, and won the national 125 GP class at 16, finishing third in the European Championship as well. Then he was old enough for GPs – a skinny, gangling 17-year-old with a Prince Valiant haircut and an ever-present sense of fun. And fast. In a 125 class dominated by seasoned veterans, Rossi adopted the nickname Rossifume in deference to the many Japanese among them, and proceeded to enjoy himself hugely. He won a single race in his first season, at Brno; in his second he was quite dominant, claiming 11 straight wins for the first trophy in his World Championship cabinet.

Graziano was a steadying force. 'I try to teach him to think about the whole race, not just passing people. And also to protect him from the pressure – he was very young, and already very famous.' Indeed so. Fortune had hit the fast-forward button, and all Rossi needed was a guiding hand while he got used to the speed.

Straight to the 250 class on a factory Aprilia, Valentino quickly adapted to double the power. The technique of riding a 250 is not so different from a 125 – smooth lines, high corner speed, good momentum and high angles of lean. 'Vale' also knew the tracks. He passed the new test to his talent with flying colours, winning five races in his first year to finish a close second overall, then dominating again in the second, adding nine more race victories.

It was an impressive display, and achieved with such *joie de vivre*. Rossi's charm meant that he could even get away with increasingly theatrical post-victory celebrations without appearing contrived.

In 1998, he proved well equal to the task of riding a 250 – with time left over for crowd-pleasing clownery.
(Henk Keulemans)

Rossi sweeps to his seventh win of the 2001 season in Portugal. Raising the stakes at almost every track, he cut 40 seconds off the previous race record at Estoril.
(Henk Keulemans)

Orchestrated by an activist core of his home-country fan club, Rossi would dress as Robin Hood at Donington Park (just down the road from Sherwood Forest and Nottingham), a mediaeval knight with an inflatable bludgeon at the Nürburgring, overlooked by the forbidding old castle; as a beach bum at home in Italy …

The real test was to come, however. The kid could ride, and he could race well. But how would he get on with a 500? Approaching 200 horsepower, using fat rear tyres to try to contain that power, riding a 500 was a very different proposition, and success in the smaller classes does not necessarily guarantee continuity.

Valentino had a lot going for him. So far, his career had been built hand in hand with the Aprilia factory. Sadly, when he wanted to move on to 500s they had no competitive machine to offer him. To their dismay, he moved to Honda, who certainly did have one – the ex-Doohan NSR500, complete with the same chief engineer and pit crew that had taken the Australian to five World Championships in a row. Led by matter-of-fact fellow-Australian Jerry Burgess, this gave the young rider a combination that all his rivals would have killed for.

Valentino did have to change his riding style, and it did take an effort. But the depth of his talent now became crystal clear, as he put the theatricals away and applied himself diligently to a task that requires courage and commitment as well as intelligence and adaptability. He had a couple of crashes along the way, but by the middle of the season you could see how his technique had developed, as he picked the bike more upright out of the corners, to use the wheelspin and drift to turn, rather than leaning it over on the tyres. He won for the first time in England, the first of two début-season victories, and even posed a distant but real threat for the championship in the closing stages. In the end, he finished second at his first attempt at the hardest and highest achievement in motorcycle racing.

After moving to 500s in 1999, Valentino introduced more sombre rituals – before every ride, he would squat by the bike to help focus his concentration. (Henk Keulemans)

The 2001 season was about Rossi and his Roman rival Max Biaggi. Here the younger rider has again just passed his Yamaha-mounted adversary, on his way to a fine victory in Britain. (Henk Keulemans)

Valentino came back in 2001 looking older, riding harder, and superbly in control of a Honda that had been revised around him.

From the first race, battle was joined between Honda's new number one rider and his fellow Italians, Capirossi (on pole position at Suzuka) and on- and off-track sparring partner Biaggi. Biaggi led. Then, at more than 135mph, Rossi tried a daring pass on the Yamaha; Biaggi responded by running wide and sticking his elbow out. Rossi was suddenly bucking and slithering on the dirt, right in front of the Suzuka grandstands. A couple of laps later he took revenge – riding almost contemptuously round the outside of Biaggi, and sticking a definitely contemptuous middle finger in the air.

Stern letters of warning came from the FIM, but nothing could stop the rivalry. Rossi definitely had the upper hand, winning the first three races. But Biaggi had his days too, and two wins by the mid-point and a solid set of other finishes had brought him to within just ten points of Valentino by the summer break (zero points, falling in the rain at Mugello, then an off-form seventh in Germany, had cost the younger rider dear).

Valentino's second half season showed yet more depth. He came back from the Eight-Hour endurance race seeming even stronger. The turning point came at the first GP, at Brno. Biaggi had tested there, Biaggi was on pole, and Biaggi was leading the race. Then, under relentless pressure from the Honda, he slid off gracefully, leaving victory to Valentino. Rossi was left with an unassailable lead, but a feeling of frustration. 'It's like somebody brings you a plate of pasta – but before you can eat it, it's taken away again.'

Father, Graziano Rossi, was a GP hero when Valentino was born. He has remained unobtrusively influential throughout his son's racing career.
(Henk Keulemans)

This was a turning point. From now on Biaggi was on his back foot, forced into ever more self-destructive feats of daring to try and regain some momentum. He fell off twice more in the same way over the next three races, simply refusing to accept the cornering limitations of his motorcycle. Rossi rode with perfect maturity, winning every remaining race but one – on the wrong tyres for the wet-and-dry Valencia round.

Rossi had something else on his side too – call it a guardian angel. Even when things went wrong for him, they'd go right. He fell off at high speed in practice at Donington – an identical crash to one that left Spanish racer Carlos Checa in a critical condition with internal injuries. Rossi walked away. Again when he went over the high-side in practice in Australia. Not even bruised, he remounted and rode back to the pits. A wasp flew into his helmet at Brno. But instead of stinging him, it flew away when he opened his visor. Even the insects were on his side.

He secured the crown with two races to spare, in Australia. He needed to finish only eighth at the sweeping and beautiful seaside circuit of Phillip Island. 'That is not the way to win the championship,' he promised, the evening before. That climactic race will be remembered as the closest ever in the 500 class. The lead changed hands over and over; at one point the Hondas of Rossi and Brazilian Alex Barros brushed tyres at 190mph, sending up a puff of smoke. Into the last tight corner, Rossi's yellow Honda dived inside Biaggi's leading red Yamaha. He held the lead round the long lefts, and though Biaggi tried everything to pull alongside down the finishing straight, Valentino clinched his first and racing's last 500cc championship by just 13 thousandths of a second.

It was an epic end to an epic era, and this new idol was a fitting figure to wear the final crown.

The champion bikes

The birth of the World Championship coincided with a drastic change in regulations – the banning of superchargers common before the war. There were other significant variations to follow – from 1958, full 'dustbin' streamlining was outlawed on safety grounds; and from 1968 came the imposition of a maximum of four cylinders and six gears. But the most significant innovation of all – almost exactly half way through the five decades of the 500 class, was the two-stroke takeover. In the end, it proved fatal.

The winner of the first championship was an all-new racer from the old British firm AJS, now part of the powerful Associated Motor Cycles group. AJS had raced a supercharged water-cooled V4 before the war, and had a supercharged water-cooled twin under development when racing was suspended. This was hastily reworked to suit the new regulations, and thus was born the air-cooled parallel twin-cylinder twin-camshaft Porcupine, so named for the spiky cylinder head finning on its horizontal cylinders. Power was around 50bhp – comparable to a modern 125 GP machine.

AJS never again carried a rider to overall victory. Rather surprisingly Norton, that great mainstay of racing, also only claimed one title – the series came a little late for the arch-exponents of fine-honed single-cylinder efficiency. Italian and Japanese machines claimed all the rest, with the Japanese big three sharing 27 (Honda with 11 wins, Yamaha ten, and Suzuki six) and Italy taking the remaining 24 (MV Agusta 18, Gilera six). By this measure, MV were the most successful single marque in the class, although Honda overtook their total tally of 139 race wins during 2000.

Masetti's Gilera, second in 1949, won the next year – the heavy and rather elaborate twin-camshaft four-cylinder offered speed and power in place of nimble handling. The design had been adapted from the pre-war supercharged Rondine, and set the template for the 'correct' design for a racing 500 four-stroke, only superseded by a more modern version of the same thing, by MV Agusta. The earth-bound flagship of a helicopter factory took over for an unbeaten 17-year run.

The Italian design was quirky by modern standards: the crankshaft carried on a separate assembly with the barrels, mounted from above in the one-piece crankcases, with a ring of bolts round the cylinder bases. With the wide valve angles popular at the time, the unit was surmounted by the two gear-driven overhead camshafts, making a fine piece of sculpture to the engineering eye.

MV were immeasurably helped in this by a lack of opposition, racing on

In 1961, his championship year, he was the greatest rider on the greatest motorbike. Here Hocking sings the MV round Mallory Park. (Nick Nicholls)

A famous frozen moment – it illustrates why the bump at the bottom of Bray Hill on the Isle of Man is called Ago's Leap. (Nick Nicholls)

In 1974, his second championship year, Read seemed fused with the MV. Note one-piece wheels, a Read innovation. (Nick Nicholls)

defiantly (even treacherously) after the other Italian factories had withdrawn en masse at the end of 1957 – an industry-wide agreement in an economic lean time for motorcycle companies. Only MV Agusta didn't join in, and raced on unmolested. In later years, MV had to fight hard against Honda, who brought their creed of multiple valves and very high revs to the big class with a highly effective four-cylinder motor. MV's response was a more compact triple; Honda were already racing a six in the 250cc class. Who knows what 500 masterpiece they might have gone on to produce had the tighter regulations of 1969 not closed down the options. Honda also withdrew in high dudgeon, and MV's reign was again untroubled.

In 1974, however, it was all but over for MV, as Phil Read swept to the last of the marque's 18 rider titles in a familiar blur of red and silver, with a new four-cylinder machine for the last stand. By now, both Yamaha and Suzuki had new four-cylinder factory 500s, and the end came suddenly for MV Agusta.

Yamaha's 1975 winner was an in-line four – literally a pair of 250cc twins laid end to end, even retaining twin crankshafts. In the coming years this basic layout would be juggled in various ways to arrive at the so-called V4 format almost universal at the end of the 500 class (the single-crankshaft Honda NSR and Swissauto V4 are exceptions).

The first challenge came from Suzuki's own twin-crankshaft square four with disc-valve induction, with the first of four rider titles (and seven consecutive manufacturer titles) in 1976. Yamaha's in-line design fought back in the hands of Kenny Roberts – but they eventually followed Suzuki's lead with their own square four. And then the big idea – splay those cylinder pairs out from each other, and you have a V4, with a lower centre of gravity, space between the cylinders for the induction, and an almost straight run for at least two out of the four exhausts. Yamaha's 0W61 of 1982 set the definition of correctness for the new kings of the 500 class.

All the same, Suzuki's old RG won twice more, and then the heretical three-cylinder NS500 Honda in 1983 (marrying torquey motocross cylinder technology with a simple single-crankshaft design previously used by DKW), before the orthodoxy was fully established.

Again it was Yamaha who won the first title with a V4, starting the modern era, as well as four years when they would swop the honours back and forth with Honda, who had responded with their single-crankshaft NSR500 in 1984. As the Nineties began, Yamaha regained supremacy for three years, and then Suzuki claimed one more crown with their own Yamaha-like twin-crank V4. And then Honda's mighty NSR, now fully developed and equipped with Mick Doohan, the best rider of his time, took over for eight years of almost total domination.

The 500 era ended, after one more Suzuki win in 2000 – the NSR claimed the final world title with a string of 11 wins for Valentino Rossi.

Five decades had seen a complete change in the machines used, and the techniques needed to ride them to the maximum. Slick tyres and effective suspension developments played their part – but the biggest difference was in the power. Approaching (possibly exceeding) 200bhp, the last 500s had almost four times as much muscle as the first.

The Honda was the best of them, where it mattered – in terms of race results. Honda had already beaten MV's total of 139 500-class GP wins, closing the account with 156. Of those, 132 went to the V4 NSR, making it handsomely the most successful single design in the 500 class.

Appendix Two

Roll of Honour

1949
1 L Graham, GB, AJS
2 N Pagani, Ita, Gilera
3 A Artesiani, Ita, Gilera

1950
1 U Masetti, Ita, Gilera
2 G Duke, GB, Norton
3 L Graham, GB, AJS

1951
1 G Duke, GB, Norton
2 Alfredo Milani, Ita, Gilera
3 U Masetti, Ita, Gilera

1952
1 U Masetti, Ita, Gilera
2 L Graham, GB, MV Agusta
3 R Armstrong, Ire, Norton

1953
1 G Duke, GB, Gilera
2 R Armstrong, Ire, Gilera
3 Alberto Milano, Ita, Gilera

1954
1 G Duke, GB, Gilera
2 R Amm, Rho, Norton
3 K Kavanagh, Aus, Norton

1955
1 G Duke, GB, Gilera
2 R Armstrong, Ire, Gilera
3 U Masetti, Ita, MV Agusta

1956
1 J Surtees, GB, MV Agusta
2 W Zeller, Ger, BMW
3 J Hartle, GB, Norton

1957
1 L Liberati, Ita, Gilera
2 B McIntyre, GB, Gilera
3 J Surtees, GB, MV Agusta

1958
1 J Surtees, GB, MV Agusta
2 J Hartle, GB, MV Agusta
3 R Dale, GB, BMW

Giants on the grid – Hailwood talks to rival Phil Read at Mallory Park, 1966. (Nick Nicholls)

German star Ernst Degner, Mike Hailwood and Gary Hocking after the 125 Ulster GP of 1959. Hocking and Hailwood shared a win apiece in the smaller classes. (Nick Nicholls)

1959
1 J Surtees, GB, MV Agusta
2 R Venturi, Ita, MV Agusta
3 B Brown, Aus, Norton

1960
1 J Surtees, GB, MV Agusta
2 R Venturi, Ita, MV Agusta
3 J Hartle, GB, Norton

1961
1 G Hocking, Rho, MV Agusta
2 M Hailwood, GB, Norton/MV Agusta
3 F Perris, GB, Norton

1962
1 M Hailwood, GB, MV Agusta
2 A Shepherd, GB, Matchless
3 P Read, GB, Norton

1963
1 M Hailwood, GB, MV Agusta
2 A Shepherd, GB, Matchless
3 J Hartle, GB, Gilera

1964
1 M Hailwood, GB, MV Agusta
2 J Ahearn, Aus, Norton
3 P Read, GB, Matchless

1965
1 M Hailwood, GB, MV Agusta
2 G Agostini, Ita, MV Agusta
3 P Driver, ZA, Matchless

1966
1 G Agostini, Ita, MV Agusta
2 M Hailwood, GB, Honda
3 J Findlay, Aus, Matchless

1967
1 G Agostini, Ita, MV Agusta
2 M Hailwood, GB, Honda
3 J Hartle, GB, Matchless

1968
1 G Agostini, Ita, MV Agusta
2 J Findlay, Aus, Matchless
3 G Marsovszky, Swz, Matchless

1969
1 G Agostini, Ita, MV Agusta
2 G Marsovszky, Swz, Linto
3 G Nash, GB, Norton

1970
1 G Agostini, Ita, MV Agusta
2 G Molloy, NZ, Kawasaki
3 A Bergamonti, Ita, Aermacchi/MV Agusta

Monza, 1966, and Agostini's first world title is just one race win away. (Maurice Büla)

1991
1 W Rainey, USA, Yamaha
2 M Doohan, Aus, Honda
3 K Schwantz, USA, Suzuki

1992
1 W Rainey, USA, Yamaha
2 M Doohan, Aus, Honda
3 J Kocinski, USA, Yamaha

1993
1 K Schwantz, USA, Suzuki
2 W Rainey, USA, Yamaha
3 D Beattie, Aus, Suzuki

1994
1 M Doohan, Aus, Honda
2 L Cadalora, Ita, Yamaha
3 J Kocinski, USA, Cagiva

1995
1 M Doohan, Aus, Honda
2 D Beattie, Aus, Suzuki
3 L Cadalora, Ita, Yamaha

1996
1 M Doohan, Aus, Honda
2 A Criville, Spn, Honda
3 L Cadalora, Ita, Honda

1997
1 M Doohan, Aus, Honda
2 T Okada, Jpn, Honda
3 N Aoki, Jpn, Honda

1998
1 M Doohan, Aus, Honda
2 M Biaggi, Ita, Honda
3 A Criville, Spn, Honda

1999
1 A Criville, Spn, Honda
2 K Roberts Jnr, USA, Suzuki
3 T Okada, Jpn, Honda

2000
1 K Roberts Jnr, USA, Suzuki
2 V Rossi, Ita, Honda
3 M Biaggi, Ita, Yamaha

2001
1 V Rossi, Ita, Honda
2 M Biaggi, Ita, Yamaha
3 L Capirossi, Ita, Honda

1971
1 G Agostini, Ita, MV Agusta
2 K Turner, NZ, Suzuki
3 R Bron, Ned, Suzuki

1972
1 G Agostini, Ita, MV Agusta
2 A Pagani, Ita, MV Agusta
3 B Kneubuhler, Swz, Yamaha

1973
1 P Read, GB, MV Agusta
2 K Newcombe, NZ, Konig
3 G Agostini, Ita, MV Agusta

1974
1 P Read, GB, MV Agusta
2 G Bonera, Ita, MV Agusta
3 T Lansivuori, Fin, Yamaha

1975
1 G Agostini, Ita, Yamaha
2 P Read, GB, MV Agusta
3 H Kanaya, Jpn, Yamaha

1976
1 B Sheene, GB, Suzuki
2 T Lansivuori, Fin, Suzuki
3 P Hennen, USA, Suzuki

1977
1 B Sheene, GB, Suzuki
2 S Baker, USA, Yamaha
3 P Hennen, USA, Suzuki

1978
1 K Roberts Snr, USA, Yamaha
2 B Sheene, GB, Suzuki
3 J Cecotto, Vnz, Yamaha

1979
1 K Roberts Snr, USA, Yamaha
2 V Ferrari, Ita, Suzuki
3 B Sheene, GB, Suzuki

1980
1 K Roberts Snr, USA, Yamaha
2 R Mamola, USA, Suzuki
3 M Lucchinelli, Ita, Suzuki

1981
1 M Lucchinelli, Ita, Suzuki
2 R Mamola, USA, Suzuki
3 K Roberts Snr, USA, Yamaha

1982
1 F Uncini, Ita, Suzuki
2 G Crosby, NZ, Yamaha
3 F Spencer, USA, Honda

1983
1 F Spencer, USA, Honda
2 K Roberts Snr, USA, Yamaha
3 R Mamola, USA, Suzuki

1984
1 E Lawson, USA, Yamaha
2 R Mamola, USA, Honda
3 R Roche, Fra, Honda

1985
1 F Spencer, USA, Honda
2 E Lawson, USA, Yamaha
3 C Sarron, Fra, Yamaha

1986
1 E Lawson, USA, Yamaha
2 W Gardner, Aus, Honda
3 R Mamola, USA, Yamaha

1987
1 W Gardner, Aus, Honda
2 R Mamola, USA, Yamaha
3 E Lawson, USA, Yamaha

1988
1 E Lawson, USA, Yamaha
2 W Gardner, Aus, Honda
3 W Rainey, USA, Yamaha

1989
1 E Lawson, USA, Honda
2 W Rainey, USA, Yamaha
3 C Sarron, Fra, Yamaha

1990
1 W Rainey, USA, Yamaha
2 K Schwantz, USA, Suzuki
3 M Doohan, Aus, Honda

Spencer's agile three-cylinder Honda was the perfect counterpoint to his quixotic talent in 1983, here at Assen, his first title year. (Henk Keulemans)

Barry Sheene ran Kenny Roberts close in 1978 – and beat him here in Sweden. (Henk Keulemans)

Other books of interest:

Wayne Rainey
His own story

by Michael Scott
ISBN 1 85960 401 3

Mick Doohan
Thunder from down under

by Mat Oxley.
ISBN 1 85960 698 9

Mike Hailwood
A motorcycle racing legend

by Mick Woollett
ISBN 1 85960 648 2

Joey Dunlop
His authorised biography

by Mac McDiarmid
ISBN 1 85960 822 1

World Superbike Winners
All the men, all the results

by Julian Ryder
ISBN 1 85960 678 4

Carl Fogarty
The complete racer

by Julian Ryder
ISBN 1 85960 641 5

Ducati People
Exploring the passion behind this legendary marque

by Kevin Ash
ISBN 1 85960 686 5